Retirement Tales

Retirement Tales

✦

Two Gringos Living in Mexico

Charlie Montemayor

Writers Club Press
New York Lincoln Shanghai

Retirement Tales
Two Gringos Living in Mexico

Writers Club Press
an imprint of iUniverse, Inc.

For information address:
iUniverse, Inc.
2021 Pine Lake Road, Suite 100
Lincoln, NE 68512
www.iuniverse.com

Individual articles in this book first appeared in
Letter from Mexico, a newsletter by Charles Montemayor

Cover Photograph by Charles Montemayor
August 2003

ISBN: 0-595-29281-X

Printed in the United States of America

Contents

Acknowledgments

The material for this book came from **Letter from Mexico,** a newsletter I wrote from July 1995 to November 2000 that was mailed out to over 140 family members and friends. These newsletters have continued beyond 2000, but I had to stop somewhere. There are many people who live in Mexico and the United States who encouraged me to put the issues of **Letter from Mexico** together in book form and publish them. I want to thank them for their encouragement and hope they buy the book.

I want to thank Ruth Steinberg and Ron Mann who both live here in Guanajuato for text-editing some of the original articles that appeared in the newsletters. I also want to thank Jan Contreras who text-edited the whole shebang and offered much valuable advice that was essential to the preparation of this book.

This adventure could never have taken place without the experiences realized from the people and places of Mexico. My life is richer and I have grown immeasurably from the events tackled, lessons learned, and broadened horizons I have realized. Mexico and her wonderful people are an enormous part of this book.

And last, but never least, I want to acknowledge the help and encouragement of my wife, Carole, even if she once joyfully dreamt that I had been arrested and thrown into a Mexican jail and she was unable to get me out. Thanks one and all.

Introduction

My wife, Carole, and I first traveled to Mexico with our two small children in 1976. On that occasion we visited Veracruz, Jalapa, and Mexico City. We thoroughly enjoyed our visit but never dreamed that we would someday live in Mexico. In 1989, I retired as Director of the Dane County (Wisconsin) Regional Planning Commission. Carole was still working as a social worker in Madison. In 1992, Carole and I took another vacation trip to Mexico. Now most people from Wisconsin choosing to visit Mexico come in the winter, and then primarily to the beach resorts to thaw out. I happen to dislike hot weather, so I voted for visiting the colonial cities in the highlands of central Mexico: Morelia, Patzquaro, Guanajuato, San Miguel de Allende, Queretaro, and Zacatecas. Carole and I spent three weeks touring them all, but it was in the garden courtyard of the Hotel Quinta Loreto in San Miguel where Carole popped the question: "When can I retire so we can move to Mexico?" We were in love—with this part of Mexico. "Well, you can retire whenever you want," said I, "but if what you want to know is what would our financial situation be if you stopped working, I can work up a spread sheet on the computer when we get home. This will tell us what our income and expenses have been for the last few years, and project ahead what they will be in the future." For Christmas that year, I presented Carole with a bound document entitled *RETIREMENT PROSPECTUS FOR CAROLE A. MONTEMAYOR: An Examination of the Feasibility and Desirability of Early Retirement in the Country of Mexico.* The plan outlined all aspects of our possibly retiring in Mexico, but also included a list of steps we should take before making such a drastic commitment.

1. We should further explore Mexico with additional visits;

2. We should pick a city and move there for a six-month trial; and,

3. If all went well, return to Madison, sell our house, and move to Mexico permanently.

Over the next few years, we accomplished our prerequisite steps and are now happily ensconced in our Mexican home in Guanajuato, Mexico. From the moment we made our decision, we knew that, above all, we didn't want to loose contact with our family and friends in the States. One reason we selected Guana-juato was that a new international airport was located nearby enabling our kids, relatives, and friends to visit. Another idea was to write a newsletter that would chronicle our adventures and help us keep in touch. We called it *Letter from Mexico—Retirement Tales of Two Gringos from Wisconsin.*

This book is a compilation of our *Letter from Mexico* from July 1995 thru November 2000. What is contained herein is written for those people who know and love Mexico or who are open to learn something of its ways and charms. It is written for all who may be interested and *con mucho amor* for Mexico.

1

July 1995

About *Letter from Mexico*

I'm not sure if this publication qualifies as an authentic "zine" or not. "Zines" are reported to be the fastest growing sector of the publishing business these days. As I understand it, the word "zine" does not come directly from "magazine" as one would expect, but rather from *fanzine*. And what is a fanzine? It's a magazine written by and for fans especially of science fiction or fantasy writing. Today, zines are narrowly focused publications usually produced through desktop publishing and have miniscule readership. We expect that all these characteristics, even possibly including the fantasy aspect, may be a part of *Letter from Mexico*.

We intend to bring you reports on retiring in Mexico. We want to share with you our little discoveries, our adventures and observations. We want to do restaurant reviews, not because we expect you to run down for lunch, but there is always the chance that we can get a free drink with our meal. We will attempt to be truthful and accurate in everything we write about Mexico with only occasional lapses such as this Vol. 1, No. 1 issue which is actually being written in Madison, Wisconsin and not in Mexico. But I think you get the idea.

House is Sold—Big Move to Mexico Next

Well friends, the Montemayor residence, placed on the market in late May, was sold June 27 to a couple from Bloomington, Indiana. We've lived in this house for the last thirty-one years, so you can see that we're not exactly nomadic. All of us in our family loved this house, especially our children. The kids thought it would be a great idea if we gave them the place. (Get real!) I hope the new owners will enjoy this house and neighborhood as much as we have.

We are now ready to embark on our long planned move to Guanajuato, Mexico. We start our move around the end of July and intend to visit some friends and relatives along the way. During our six-month trial visit during the winter of 1993-94, we met some wonderful people who were always willing to lend us a hand in getting settled, so it's not as if we are embarking on a far side lunar landing. Our friend, Elisa Young, told us about a house we were familiar with and we agreed to rent it. Later, we would like to purchase a house, but renting enables us to take our time in looking for a place without feeling rushed.

Where is Guanajuato?

Located in central Mexico 180 miles east of Guadalajara, Mexico's second largest city, and 231 miles north of Mexico City, Guanajuato is considered by many to be the actual geographic center of Mexico. On a mountaintop a few miles outside the city is an enormous statue of *Cristo Rey*, Christ the King, marking the "center" of Mexico for the thousands of *peregrinos,* pilgrims, who annually come to worship. Some people will tell you that the geographic center of the country is actually near San Louis Potosi, the capital of the adjoining northern State, but suffice it that Guanajuato is about as central as you can get. Guanajuato is a city of about 80,000 people although some reports say it's 110,000. It is the capital of the Sate of Guanajuato and home of the State University. People ask me if we will be close to any dangerous areas. Well, Oklahoma City, site of the bombing of the Muir Federal Building, is 1,017 miles from Guanajuato as compared with 910 miles from Madison. Guanajuato is also 1,014 miles from Chiapas, home of the Zapatistas rebels, so you see how we are managing to keep our distance from some of the world's trouble spots.

The city is 6,600 feet above sea level and is surrounded by mountains that the Mexicans call hills; adjoining it to the east are the Sierra de Guanajuato Mountains. To the south is the Bajio, which means lowland in Spanish, although it is over a mile high. The area of the Bajio flattens out to provide a fertile and productive agricultural area when the land is irrigated. It is sometimes referred to as the breadbasket of Mexico, but those of us who have taken advanced courses in geography and Spanish know that this actually means *tortilla* basket.

Why Guanajuato?

After our visits to the other colonial cities of Mexico we fell most in love with Guanajuato. There is something magical about this hidden gem in the central highlands of the country. The architecture, the steep topography, the attractive cityscapes, the winding cobblestone streets and little pedestrian walkways that climb up the steep canyon walls; the churches, the old haciendas, and the aqueducts combine to make Guanajuato an unusually attractive town. It has oddities, legends and an amazing history, and it has a certain air of isolation about it. Built in 1559 along the Guanajuato River, which has subsequently been diverted after the city suffered a devastating flood in 1905, the old riverbed provided an excellent roadway for a *subterráneo* that winds throughout the city. The many stone arches and buildings that spanned this old river give it a tunnel-like appearance, and new tunnels have been built that connect the *subterráneo* with other parts of the city. As a retired city and regional planner, I am unaware of another city in the world quite like it.

For people like us who like a temperate climate, Guanajuato is superb. Some people say that San Diego has the best climate in America. In the coldest month of the year, Guanajuato has an average temperature that is two degrees warmer than San Diego; and during the warmest month of the year, Guanajuato has a temperature about two degree cooler than San Diego. I believe it was The National Geographic Magazine that stated Guadalajara and Nairobi, Africa have the best climates in the world. Guanajuato may not be exactly the same, but it is a close second.

Although largely unknown to North Americans, the city is visited by many Mexicans because of its historical significance to Mexico. The city sponsors many cultural events in music, art and dance, and fiesta days, making it a lively place for the residents and visitors. One thing that Carole and I like about Guanajuato is her similarity to Madison. Both are state capitals, have large universities and do not have any polluting industries. In the case of Guanajuato, the steep topography constrains development making it a compact environment that probably never will have much in the way of industrial development. The city has several silver and gold mines that are still being worked even though some of them have been in operation since the XVI Century. Rather surprisingly, the mines look very park like, and although they are very old they are quite clean and pleasant to visit. It is often said here that at one time the mines of Guanajuato produced one-third of all the silver ore produced in the world.

Americans in Mexico

While there are a number of Americans, along with some Canadians and British folks living in Guanajuato, there are not many. About 50 miles to the east is San Miguel de Allende, which has a lot of Anglos. One magazine article I read said that in San Miguel you might see George and Barbara Bush or Lee Iococa who sometimes visit there. On one occasion Carole and I saw Kenny Rogers in a restaurant. We learned from a waiter that he was visiting his mother who lives there year round. Well, that's not the scene in Guanajuato, which is fine with us. But throughout Mexico there are a lot of Americans. According to the U.S. Statistical Abstract there are 495,000 Americans living in Mexico not including 300,000 tourists. That comes out to 1 out of every 502 Americans live in Mexico. There are more U.S. citizens living in Mexico than live in Wyoming. And soon there will be two more Americans living in Mexico.

We've spent almost all of our lives in Wisconsin, thirty-two years in Madison, so we are not exactly on the run. We both truly love Wisconsin and Madison, especially the people there. We plan on returning for visits with our kids, relatives and friends, so it's not as if we have left the face of the earth. We hope that *Letter from Mexico* helps convey our enthusiasm and interest in our move south. An important reason for picking Guanajuato is that we wanted a beautiful and interesting place like this that would be attractive to our family and friends to visit. The Leon/Guanajuato airport (BJX International) is a little over four hours from O'Hare in Chicago and thirty minutes to our home Guanajuato. After we are settled, we hope our friends will come to visit. As they say in Mexico: *Mi casa es su casa* or is it, *cum si cum sa*. No, I think it is *cum si mi casa*. I always got those mixed up since those Doris Day movies. I can't say when the next *Letter from Mexico* will arrive at your mailbox because we will be pretty busy getting settled, but until then, *Adios amigos!*

Charlie and Carole

2

October 1995

Bureaucratic Barricade, The Economy, Police Encounter, Chepa, *Casas Populares,* Home Improvement

Bureaucratic Barricade Slows But Fails to Halt Move of Intrepid Pair to Mexico

It all seems so simple and laughable now, but we had ourselves a nasty complication in our move to Mexico. Back in the fall of 1993, Carole and I moved to Guanajuato, Mexico for a six-month trial visit to see if we would like to retire there. Having read various books on living in Mexico, we learned that Americans and other foreigners were welcome to come as tourists or, if they met certain requirements, as residents with an FM-3 permit issued by the Mexican General Consul closest to their home. This document allows you to bring your household goods into the country without paying duty. That was exactly the plan for us, so we applied for and received our FM-3. We loaded up our Ford, and headed south. Our trial visit to Guanajuato convinced us that we would like to live in Mexico year round. We returned to Wisconsin to sell our house and arrange our affairs. Admittedly, we were aware that the FM-3 had to be renewed each year and that you could only leave for periods of no more than six months at a time, but saw no ensuing problem; we thought, even if it takes us more than six months to sell our house, we'll just apply for a new permit. Well, no ERROR lights flashed on when we made that assumption.

We found ourselves with our house sold, our household goods stored in a moving company warehouse in Madison, and camped out at the home of Mike and Maureen Torphy. However, we were now informed by, well I'll call him Fernando Functionary, office of the Chicago General Consul of the Republic of Mexico, that we were not entitled to a re-issue of our FM-3 permit. If we wished to move to Mexico, we would have to pay duty on all our household possessions.

Sr. Functionary said he understood the duty to be 32.5% of the value, and that we should contact the Mexican Embassy in Washington, D.C. to get the details. There didn't seem to be much choice, so I called the Embassy in Washington to find out how we pay the duty so that we could move our goods. The woman I spoke to explained that I needed to have a customs broker and gave me the phone number of three customs brokers in Nuevo Laredo, Mexico who could assist us. I don't think she knew, as we later learned, that they had just changed the phone numbers in that growing city. The first number she gave me was to a FAX machine. My second call was to a hardware store and the third call was to a *farmacia*, pharmacy. Except for the FAX machine everyone was very polite and tried to be helpful, but they spoke very little English and I speak very little Spanish, especially under pressure. The call to the Mexican *farmacia* with its scratchy phone connection had its moments. "I'm calling from Madison Wisconsin," I said. "You wan medicine?" came the reply. "No, I am looking for a customs broker because I want to ship our household goods to Mexico." I couldn't understand what she was saying, and all I could think about was that line from the movie, *Treasure of Sierra Madre*, where the bandito sneers at Humphrey Bogart, "We don wan your stinking guds." After some time I finally understood I was talking to someone at a pharmacy. I knew I needed help so I called Hector Montemayor, a cousin of mine who lives in Piedras Negras just across the border from Eagle Pass, Texas—someone I had not seen in fifty years. Hector remembered who I was and said he would seek some advice from some local customs brokers he knew. When he got back to me he said that his friend had told him it was ridiculous for us to pay duty on our household goods and that the Mexican Consulate can make an exception and reissue our FM-3 permit.

Calling the Consulate of Mexico in Chicago can be a daunting task. It would appear that some efficiency expert has analyzed every conceivable question that could be asked of a Consul and determined and recorded an appropriate response in both English and Spanish so that the entire operation can be conducted by pressing buttons on a touch tone phone without any human involvement whatsoever. Every question save one, however, and that question is: "Could I please talk to a real <u>person</u>?!" There didn't seem to be any way to talk to anyone except with Fernando Functionary to whom I had already spoken and who had already informed me that I would have to pay the import duties on our household goods.

Getting a new FM-3 seemed like a lost cause. Lost cause? Lost cause? Did I say lost cause? What about Tom Hecht's run for congress against the Republican landslide in the last election? What about our feeble efforts to lend a hand in that doomed campaign? Hey, wasn't Tom Hecht's dad, Dr. Rudi Hecht, Honorary

Mexican Consul in Madison? Yes! Maybe Dr. Hecht could help. A call to Dr. Hecht revealed that as an "honorary" consul he couldn't do much to help us, but he could give me the direct telephone number of the General Consul's office in Chicago. There, I got a hold of the Assistant General Consul, Mercedes Valesques de Mew. Perhaps with my long and special relationship with cats, I would be able to successfully plead my case to Srta. de Mew. Unfortunately, her response was the same as Fernando's—that the FM-3 is issued only once to a person. "But I understand that exceptions are made," I said. She finally agreed to call Mexico City to see if they would grant such an exception.

I thought it might be helpful to apply some positive reinforcement so I faxed her copies of some very nice letters of reference written by Juan Jose Lopéz, Board Chairman of the United Migrant Opportunity Services, and Lupe Martinez, CEO of this organization. UMOS is a very successful organization that helps migrant workers in Wisconsin. I had served on the board, and Juan and Lupe offered to write letters, in Spanish, on my behalf just in case we got into trouble in our first move to Mexico. I also contacted U.S. Senator Feingold's home office to see if they would call the Mexican Consulate and support my plea. Staff at the Senator's office said that they were reluctant to get involved in international affairs, but I pressed them for help nonetheless. [I later found out that the Mexican Consul was not at all pleased with this intervention from a U.S. Senator's office.] The good news, however, was that in view of the fine things reported about me in the letters of reference from Juan and Lupe, the government of the Republic of Mexico would grant an exception and we could have a new FM-3 permit. Srta. de Mew said I should submit evidence of sufficient income, letters of reference from our Chief of Police, and a letter from our doctor indicating that we had no communicable diseases.

For a small fee the Madison Police Department will furnish you a visa letter. I have always regarded the Madison PD as one of the nation's finest, but was somewhat dismayed to read the opening of this form letter that was going to get us into Mexico. It read: "We have been unable to locate a record of physical arrest on file for the person whose name is shown above. This does not preclude the possibility that some arrest may have occurred, etc. etc. etc.." Gheez, what kind of a letter is that?

Well, at least we shouldn't have a problem with the letter from our doctor. We've both been going to the same medical group for decades, and I assumed they should be able to match the Madison police department in <u>not</u> finding any record of a communicable disease. As it would happen, Carole's doctor retired the very day we were to come in for the letter. My doctor came to the rescue and offered to prepare letters for both of us, however we needed to have TB skin tests and chest X-rays. Considering all the communicable diseases out there I guess we were pretty lucky that this is all we had to be tested for. As it turned out, Carole's skin test came up positive and we had to await the radiologist's report. Many thoughts raced through my mind at Carole's newly discovered disease. What I was thinking was that she should never have become a social worker. Let some one else work with the lame, the halt, the blind, the poor who obviously "infected" her with disease, pestilence, and deprivation of every kind. And having lived together all these years, why hadn't I tested positive? I wondered if we could find some nice TB sanitarium where we could spend our few remaining years together. It seemed like it took forever, but the radiologist's report finally came through, and he gave her a clean bill of health. Hurray, we're on our way!

Back to Chicago and the counter of Fernando Functionary. "Yes", he said, "I understand that you have been granted an exception on your FM-3 permit, but what is it that you have in your hand—is that a list, is that a list of things you want to move to Mexico?" "Yes," I answered, "it is a detailed list with brand names, model and serial numbers of all appliances, and a description of the con-tents of each box or container as required of persons moving their household goods to Mexico under an FM-3 permit." He informed me that while I had a new FM-3 permit, that didn't mean I could move our household goods into the country. But why, I wanted to know would I want an FM-3 if it were not to move our possessions? I was trying not to get mad because I knew that only encourages people like Fernando. After a long discussion, he consented to let me talk to Mercedes Valesques de Mew who seemed to be warmer and more under-standing. Fernando reminds me of a county register of deeds in a small county in Wisconsin about whom they tell this story. It seems that a new father rushed into the Courthouse one day a few minutes before closing time. He knew it was late but he urgently wanted to register the birth of his new baby boy because he and his family were moving out of state to live with the child's grandmother. He wanted to get the birth certificate registered before they moved. So when he entered the Courthouse, he asked where the Register of Deeds was located. They told him it was on the third floor but that he would have to hurry because the Register was extremely punctilious and correct in everything he did and that it would be difficult to arrive there before closing time. The new dad raced up the steps and arrived at the office just as the hands on the clock struck five. Breath-lessly, the new father stated that he needed to get his son's birth certificate regis-tered. The Register of Deeds explained that he was sorry but the office closed promptly at five o'clock and that he could not register the certificate except during <u>official</u> office hours. After continued pleas from the father the Register explained that if he were to record the certificate when the office was not <u>officially</u> open his son would very likely be a technical bastard for the rest of his life. "And you wouldn't want that for your son, would you?" he said. "Heck no", the father replied, "cause downstairs that's what they told me you were!"

Well, as I said, Mercedes was more sympathetic and finally agreed to call the Mexican Embassy in Washington to obtain approval. After several hours, I got word that we were approved. Hurray! We're on our way!

By this time, the Consulate was closing, and Fernando said he would FedEx the documents to the Torphy residence in Madison, and that they would arrive Saturday morning. On Saturday morning, we packed up our van all set to begin our long journey and new adventure, but first a trip to the Federal Express office in Madison to pick up the documents. The lady at Federal Express said they didn't have anything for us and that their computer showed nothing arriving from anywhere in the city of Chicago to our ZIP code in Madison. We had already stayed two weeks at the Torphys and we felt it was time to move on to somewhere else, so we sadly left Madison. We would drive to nearby Janesville and stay with our longtime friend, Nancy Fennema. At least this was forty miles closer to the Mexican Consulate in Chicago where we would probably have to camp. Great news when we arrived at Nancy's! Federal Express had called the Torphys and said our package had arrived twenty minutes after we had left their office. Hurray, now we're really on our way!

We had enjoyable visits with my sister, Bertha Burghard, her husband, Rollie; with Rod and Lois Dittmer in Paducah where I hit a $400 jackpot on a riverboat casino; and with Neal and Inez Hartwell in their home in the Ozarks of Arkansas. I first met Neal when I was doing city planning in Green Bay. Even though he came from a long line of suburban Milwaukee Republicans, he and I got involved in the "Joe Must Go" movement that attempted to recall Senator Joseph McCarthy. McCarthy was born and reared just forty miles from Green Bay. The leaders of the recall movement thought it would be a great coup to have a strong recall effort on his doorsteps. Neal and I were probably lucky that **we** weren't recalled from this planet. Our search for recall petition signers came to an end when one irate Republican came after me with a hammer. This was not your country club-type Republican.

Finally we arrived at Carole's sister's house in Dallas where we took it easy for a few days and prepared our entry into Mexico. The next day we made our way to Laredo and prepared ourselves for crossing the border. In Mexico, they refer to the border as *la frontera*. And "frontier" is the way we regarded it. We braced ourselves for a crossing of this administrative and bureaucratic frontier. What else could Mexican bureaucracy throw at us; perhaps some new regulation calling for strip searches for Americans like us? What does "bend over" sound like in Spanish. I couldn't have been more wrong. The whole operation was efficient and reasonably quick as they stamped all our documents and sent us on our way. The closer to Mexico, the easier it was.

We decided to avoid the toll road, and found the two-lane highway to Monterrey not very busy. We stopped at a small town to eat and were surprised at the low cost of an excellent meal in a clean and attractive restaurant—six dollars for the two of us served by an attentive young man with a fresh white shirt and a bow tie. (Carole does some editing of these articles and added "and pants" to the end of the previous sentence. How many of you readers out there would have thought that my description of the waiter meant that the waiter served us with no pants?)

We found ourselves turning in late that afternoon at a recommended motel in Matehuala, a town between Saltillo and San Luis Potosi. Las Palmas was a big motel with a nice restaurant and only a few guests. The next morning, Carole and I were finishing our breakfast of fresh fruit, *juevos rancheros*, bacon and tortillas, when I said I would like to go to the desk to pick up a local newspaper. When I returned to the table where I thought Carole was sitting I sat down and, without looking up, told Carole that the morning papers hadn't arrived yet. A man came up behind me, placed a firm grip on my shoulder and uttered something sternly at me in Spanish. I suspect what he said was: "What are you doing with my wife?" Looking up, I discovered that I had picked the wrong table and was met with laughter from Carole, the waiter, the husband and a great smile from my new breakfast companion.

As we entered the State of Guanajuato we saw enormous thunderheads ahead of us. The shortest and most spectacular approach to Guanajuato is through the historic towns of Dolores Hidalgo and Valenciana. But this requires driving through some rugged mountains on roads whose design engineers never heard of shoulders. I have a *Landforms Map of Mexico* on my wall prepared for the Geographic Branch of the Office of Naval Research that describes the geographic provinces of Mexico. Sierra de Guanajuato is a mountain range between the Sierra Madre Oriental and Sierra Madre Occidental. The description of the Oriental begins: "This province contains some of the most spectacular scenery in North America." I don't know if Erwin Raise, the cartographer who produced this map, had this stretch of road in mind but I think he would have been impressed. At any rate, we decided this time to take the longer route, which goes through the historic town of San Miguel de Allende and is less mountainous. Good thing too, because we encountered a downpour of such intensity that in various road-cuts, the water cascaded over the rocks with enough force to form a stream of water as if it were shooting out of a pipe.

The rain stopped as we pulled up to our new home in Marfil, an old Colonia part of the city of Guanajuato. In our previous visits we had always come in the winter which is the dry season. But on this occasion everything was green. It was as if we had arrived at the Emerald City. Our friends, Dolores Rylee and Elisa Young had put together a little food package so that we didn't have to go shopping for food; we were *muy contentos*.

The Economy

The Mexican economy took a major hit at the end of last year (1994) with a peso devaluation of about 50%. I expected to see a lot more poverty and despair than what we had observed on our previous visit here. What we actually have been seeing in Guanajuato since our arrival is something quite different. There is no question in my mind that people here are hurting economically. A friend, Margarita Acevedo, who owns several houses here, says people in Mexico City are really mad at the government. We find that people shake their heads in disbelief when the subject of the devaluation comes up. What is amazing though is the feverish activity and the enormous energy that is going into fixing everything up in Guanajuato. A large part of this is preparation for the annual International Cervantino Festival that brings people from all over the world to Guanajuato to enjoy music, dance, theater, literary lectures, and visual arts.

The buildings that front virtually every plaza in town are being patched up with cement and painted. New cobblestones and paving stones are being installed to replace missing ones. Parks and fountains are being refurbished. Most of this comes under a program of urban image-enhancement, but there are rural programs as well. The government has ordered improvements to private property but permits owners to stretch out repayment for the work by placing the cost on the owner's property tax bill. A new tunnel is being added to this city's unusual underground transportation system. A large new convention hotel has been completed. The city and state I'm sure are strapped for cash but continue to support the arts through music, museums and other cultural programs. The Governor, who is from the centrist-conservative PAN party said he would not cut funding for cultural activities. Ah, what a strange and different world this third world is. Driving through the narrow streets of the city is like encountering one of those scenes from a Peter Bruegel painting—scores of workers on wooden scaffolding and ladders can be seen fixing up buildings and others improving streets.

The News, which is an English language newspaper published in Mexico City, recently reported that the national government has avoided a policy of reviving the economy through public works for fear of increasing the deficits and fueling inflation. The Guanajuato State government, in contrast, seems to have gone all out for public works. Towns that get to be 450 years old need a little maintenance work once in awhile, and it also puts a lot of people to work.

On a previous visit to Mexico I once met a tour group from Boston. A nice lady from Cape Cod asked me how I could stand living in a place where there are beggars on the street and so much poverty. I think there is less visible poverty in Guanajuato than other cities in Mexico but it, too, has its share. At the time of the inquiry, however, I responded that even in affluent Madison, one encounters panhandlers on State Street. She and her friends agreed that the same was true in Boston. But I now think that this was the wrong response to her question. Poverty is a condition that surrounds us in varying degrees and avoiding areas where it exits doesn't make it go away. After all, it's still there even if it isn't staring you in the face. I find I get a real lift in seeing the kind of community improvement programs going on here. Pedro, who works at the Ferranti Packard Transformer factory, a division of Rolls Royce, comes once a week to take care of our garden. (I know this doesn't have anything to do with the story I'm writing, but don't you like the idea that someone from Rolls Royce is taking care of my garden.) Living with his extended family not far from our place, Pedro's street has a paved surface much better than ours. (Our street is part cobblestone and part dust.) On Pedro's street, the paving work was done by the people living on the street with the government paying for the cement and gravel. I think that's pretty neat. In spite of economic hardship there is a much higher percentage of intact families in Mexico; even when things are tough, people here seem to know how to have a good time. And that's not bad.

Police Encounter

What I know about Latin American police departments is largely what I have learned by watching American movies. The police drive around in white pick-up trucks with several cops in the back and two in the front. They look more like soldiers than policemen. The street that Carole and I live on is Camino Antigua. Our house is about 300 feet from the intersection with Camino Real, the royal highway of Spanish colonial days.

Camino Antigua makes a bend in front of our place and winds its way down to run along side the Guanajuato River, whereas Camino Real connects up the various old haciendas that sit cheek to jowl along its length. This road was used by pack trains for transporting gold and silver ore to the ore processing haciendas in times past. One has the feeling that as old as Camino Real is, Camino Antigua was carrying traffic long before the first Spaniard set foot here in the 1540's and that indigenous people traversed this route for a thousand years just as they do today. Passing in front of our place are a lot of pedestrians, religious processions, burros, some trucks and cars, but by comparison with other vehicular ways, it is a fairly tranquil street.

A couple of weeks ago, early in the morning, I got up to go to the little stores that are at the "T" intersection of Camino Antiguo and Camino Real. Right at the intersection are two stores joined to each other, *Miscelanea Yussy,* that sells fruit and vegetables and *La Gloria Carniceria*, a meat market. Just as I turned the bend from our house, I saw a shiny white pickup truck come to a halt at the intersection. Two policemen jumped out of the back of the truck while two others remained inside the cab and two in the truck bed These policemen wore dark blue uniforms with shiny black combat boots and held their AK-47's in a port arms position. Their caps looked like the type of hats one sees in pictures of German police and not dissimilar to the ones that were once proposed for the guards in the Nixon White House. If this is still unclear, they look like what you would expect to see in a performance of the Student Prince, only they are blue-black in color. We know the people who own and work in these two stores, and I couldn't imagine a reason for police action here. One policeman was standing at the open front door with his machine gun held at the ready while his companion went inside. I didn't want to get too close, but I was curious to see what was happening. In a few minutes the policemen left *Miscelanea Yussy* with a large bottle of Squirt.

Chepa

Chepa didn't exactly come with the house but she was the maid here when Elisa and Derek Young lived in our house and was recommended to us by them. She helps us out seven hours a day three days a week. She cleans, cooks and irons our clothes and when we get a laundry machine she will do the wash. Chepa is probably a little less than five feet tall, has slightly graying hair, dark skin, very white teeth, and speaks only Spanish. I know this sounds like wishful thinking on our part, but she seems to really like what she does. She sings and hums all day long.

Carole remarked the other day that Chepa hums happy little tunes while she cleans out the toilet bowls. She takes the bus in from Santa Teresa, a village that is about seven miles from our house. She brings us homemade tortillas that taste better than the ones made in the *tortilleria* on Camino Real. We always thought these tasted so much better than the packaged ones we used to buy in Madison. Conversations with Chepa tend to consist of a lot of *si*'s and smiles. Hopefully, when our Spanish improves we will get to know her better. Anyone who has reared seven daughters and smiles all day knows something that should be worth learning.

Casas Populares

The house we live in has a *terraza* over the garage that is our favorite spot in the house. Unlike the houses on the *Panorámica* and so many of the houses in Guanajuato, it lacks a spectacular view of the city, but the *terraza* is a nice place to have a drink, play a game of cards, or just watch the people passing by. One of the nice social conventions observed here is the polite greeting of *buenos dias, buenas tardes*, or *buenas noches*. This is done with a slight nodding of the head. I suppose it is a remnant of a bow. It is amazing to me how this little cordiality gives a feeling of graciousness among the people in Mexico. The nice thing is that visitors such as we can partake in this civility as well.

One Sunday morning I was sitting out on the *terraza,* and probably because there was no one walking by, I started to look across the street over the rooftops, past Mexico Highway 110, and up the enormous slope that faces Marfil. I hadn't paid particular attention before to a string of houses that were just on this side of the crest of the hill, but on this particular Sunday, I could see two white dots bouncing up and down. Their movement synchronized such that when one went up the other went down. I couldn't make out what these white dots were, so I got out my binoculars to get a better look. It turned out that the dots were two small girls dressed in their go-to-church dresses jumping rope.

I've been told that the *Club Campestre,* which is the local country club owns the land where these little girls played and that the string of houses belongs to squatters. There are no roads to this little settlement; just a path, and everything from water to white dresses has to be carried up this enormous hill through human effort. I have watched this part of the hill at night and have never seen a light, so I suspect that it lacks electricity and public water supply. One house at the end of the row has a TV antenna, however, which is hard to fathom. On this particular Sunday, when I first noticed the two bouncing white dots, I saw two larger people stop by the little girls. Soon they were all descending the hill on an angular path probably on their way to church. I can't be certain, but it looked as if the two white dots were skipping or hopping on their way down.

Home Improvement

I wasn't able to bring but a fraction of my Madison workshop to Mexico, but I did manage to bring about five boxes of tools and hardware items. One of my first projects was to install two towel bars in the bathroom. Although the house is fairly large the largest bathroom, the one with the tub and shower, is quite small. Moreover, it has only one towel rack that is no more than a foot long. I was unable to find a towel bar in any of the hardware stores in Guanajuato so I drove to nearby Silao where I found what I was looking for. With my electric drill and a carbide bit, I proceeded to drill screw holes into the masonry wall. While drilling the third hole for one end of the bar I thought my drill hit a rock, because I felt some stiff resistance. Soon water started to squirt out at me and, of course, I realized that I had struck a copper water pipe. What it was doing there only God and the *maestro* who built this house know. I viewed this as pretty serious because our house was blessed with a triple sized water tank on the roof of the house. There is a shut off valve on the roof but getting up there requires a small jump from an iron spiral staircase that leads to a second-story detached *bodega*, or store room, to the roof of the house. If I missed a jump like that I knew I would never be able to explain to Carole why I even tried. So I got out the telephone directory we had purchased a year ago and which is now out of print and unavailable at any price, to find a plumbing shop. The Telmex phone directory is sometimes referred to in Mexico as *el libro del los muertos*, the book of the dead. Many of the people listed in the book are no longer living but continue to be listed as owners of phones with new owners inheriting the line. Dead or alive, not a single *plomero* was listed in the yellow pages. I even checked a Spanish-English dictionary to see if there might be another name for plumber. I know that Guanajuato has plumbers because I have seen their shops. Why they do not have telephones listed for their business remains a mystery. It could be they don't want to be bothered, but more likely, they don't want to pay for a commercial listing with the phone company; or maybe they don't want to pay for a telephone at all. While I am conducting this search for a plumber, water is leaking onto the floor of the bathroom.

The only thing I could think of was to run over to Jack Moore's house to see if he knew of a nearby plumber that could actually be called. Out on the street I ran into José Carabajo, our friendly realtor friend, who has been showing us houses for the last several weeks. José worked for the C&NW RR in Chicago at one time and speaks some English. Later, he became warden of the Guanajuato State Penitentiary but lost this job when the PAN political party beat out the PRI. "Hi, Charrley, how are you today?" I'm not very affable under pressure so I just blurted out that I had a big problem. José said that he had his associate, Juaquin, with him, and that Juaquin could fix anything in a house. This neat little man who looked and sounded like he could teach accounting in a business school followed me into the house with a tool box that opened up into four levels and had a small version of every possible tool needed in a house. He took out a small chisel and neatly cut away a section of wall until he cleared an area around the copper pipe. By now the water was squirting in his face and he pronounces one word: "*Fácil!*" I asked Carole. "What did he say?" and he amplified by adding the word: "*Símple!*" I had trouble comprehending this because the water was now squirting on the both of us. Carole yelled out, "He is saying that it is **simple.**"

Juaquin explained that it would be neither necessary to turn off the water or to solder the pipe. He took out a drill and proceeded to enlarge the hole in the copper water pipe, which struck me as insane. Now the water was really pouring out. He then proceeded to screw a small screw into the opening. The leak stopped immediately and completely. He inquired whether I had any *geso*, which is a plaster patch in powder form. I did, and so he neatly patched the hole. I asked how much for his work; he said I should pay him whatever I wanted. I hate it when they say that. The job didn't take him very long, but I looked at his shirt and my shirt and thought about that triple sized water tank on the roof. I gave him sixty pesos, about $10. He then asked if I wanted him to install the towel bars that I had intended to install. He accomplished this quickly along with hooking up an additional telephone for us that I couldn't do by myself because I didn't know how to pound small staples into what appeared to me to be a solid concrete wall. For Juaquin, it was *muy símple.*

3

November 1996

Furniture Arrives; Home Improvement; Chepa Invites the Monts to a Fiesta; A Visit to the Monts, Dolores Hidalgo, San Miguel de Allende, Apaseo el Alto, Queretero; Carlos's First Law of Living in Mexico—*It's Not Wrong, It's Different;* Season's Greetings to All

Furniture Arrives, We start to Settle In

The furniture from our Madison house was neatly packed in three large plywood crates measuring 4' × 8' × 8' and fastened together with drywall screws. I explained to the movers back in Madison that I didn't think their moving van could negotiate the streets of Guanajuato. The folks at Mayflower Van Lines explained that they could place the large wooden crates on a smaller flatbed truck. Of course, we worried that our goods would be lost, a crate would fall off, or Mexican Customs would want to examine the contents of each crate and, finding that I had mislabeled a box, return the stuff to Wisconsin.

After several weeks we received a call from the moving company saying that our household goods were in Mexico City ready to be moved to Guana-juato—when would we like them? We were a little chagrined that by shipping our goods to Mexico City they had overshot us by 200 miles, but I suppose in Mexico, all roads lead to Mexico City. We were told to fax them a notarized copy of our FM-3 forms. I thought the bank, where we had opened an account, would be a good place to get the documents notarized, however, the folks at the bank told me that we would have to go to a lawyer who was a notary public. Many lawyers in Guanajuato have their offices located in the *Plaza de Baratillo*. This is a small plaza in the center of town with a handsome Florentine fountain said to have been given to the City by the Emperor Maximillian. The word *baratillo* means bargain, sale, or the like. The Plaza got its name from the auctions and sales conducted there, although no such activity presently takes place.

The word "bargain" didn't apply to the notarization work we needed—one hundred sixty pesos for two documents. That's more than what Chepa makes for three days work in our house. This may explain why lawyers in Mexico have higher incomes than do medical doctors. With this heavy-duty legal work completed and the FAX sent to Transcontainer, Mayflower's Mexican affiliate, our household goods soon arrived. We were happy to receive our furnishings, and I was pleased at the idea that we were the first Americans to have their goods arrive in Guanajuato on the Mayflower. I lent the movers my electric screwdriver. They thought it was pretty neat and its use speeded the unpacking. The movers carefully checked to see that only the boxes we had packed were in the crates and all contents matched the manifest. I don't think any Customs officials had ever examined the contents of the boxes. Nothing was missing or broken, save for a slightly dented pewter bowl. Our only problem was how to fit our furniture into a furnished house. The house we were renting has a *bodega*, or storage room, built over a detached laundry room and accessed by a metal spiral staircase. Any notion that I may have ever had of wanting to be a lighthouse keeper vanished as I carried boxes up these steps to the storage area.

Chepa Invites the Monts to a Fiesta

A few weeks ago our maid, Chepa, invited us to her home in Santa Teresa for a confirmation party for her ten-year-old grandson, Carlos Abraham. Although we had Cervantes Festival tickets for a concert at the church in Valenciana (which was advertised as exceptional), consultation with our friend Elisa Young (who shares Chepa's services with us), told us that missing Chepa's party would definitely be in bad form. Chepa's pig had been butchered for the occasion, and she would be serving *carnitas,* a delicious way of preparing pork. Chepa's pig is not one of those corn-fed monsters that are all fat. No, this pig eats the same kind of food we eat, only later in the day when the table scraps are collected from our house for his dinner. We decided that we could leave the concert early and still make this party. We had asked Chepa what Carlos Abraham would like for a confirmation present and she said: "Oh, a religious medal would be nice." We settled on a junior soccer ball and a Chicago Bull's cap. For some reason, the Bulls are popular in this area. I am happy to report that Carlos did not lack for religious medals and was very pleased with the athletic gear we gave him.

Chepa has a nice house with a large veranda where several tables were arranged. People kept coming and Chepa, with the help of her daughters, kept bringing out platters of food, sauces, beer and soft drinks. I asked Chepa how many people she had invited and she smiled, shrugged her shoulders and told us she didn't know. They kept coming all afternoon. I sat next to a University professor whose field was labor law. He didn't actually know Chepa, but his wife worked with one of her daughters, and so they were invited. As busy as Chepa was, she had time to sit down and talk with us. I asked her if she intended to raise another pig; she wasn't sure. I suggested that this time she should raise a goat, so that she could prepare the famous Mexican dish, *cabrito*, kid. She laughed and proceeded to tell us a story about a priest that came to live in Santa Teresa to serve the parish. The villagers were expected to prepare some special meals at various times for the priest. I don't know if they didn't like him or simply didn't have enough money, but Chepa said they cooked up dog and told him it was *cabrito*. The padre grew to like this dish, so it was prepared with some frequency. In time they grew fond of their priest and were saddened to learn he was being transferred to another parish. For his final meal in Santa Teresa, they decided to feed him real *cabrito*. The priest told them that the meat was good but not quite as good as the *cabrito* they use to cook for him.

A Visit to the Monts

Dolores Hidalgo

Rod Dittmer and his wife, Lois, from Paducah, Kentucky, arrived just in time to catch the end of the 23rd International Cervantino Festival, held in October of each year. We enjoyed their visit that included side trips to several nearby towns, all of which abound in Spanish colonial and Mexican history.

About 33 miles from the city of Guanajuato, across the breathtaking Sierra Guanajuato, is Dolores Hidalgo, known as the cradle of Mexican independence. On September 15, 1810, Father Miguel Hidalgo proclaimed Mexico's independence from Spain. This ceremony is reenacted in Guanajuato and throughout the Republic each year. We attended the celebration with the Dittmer's—it was very moving, and, perhaps, you might say exciting. The program ended with a splendid fireworks display when rockets are shot over the heads of the crowd. Facing the attractive central plaza in Dolores is a grand colonial church. The plaza has several ice cream vendors who sell some unique, if not bizarre, ice cream flavors: alfalfa, avocado, tequila, shrimp, and *mole* ice cream, to mention just a few. I'm older and more conservative now and so passed up the exotic flavors choosing vanilla with fresh pineapple and pistachio nuts. The ice cream vender has a scrapbook with pictures of himself selling his ice cream to visitors from around the world. He informed me that the Japanese especially liked the shrimp ice cream. His scrapbook also included a restaurant review on his ice cream stand from a Los Angeles newspaper. He was very proud.

Dolores Hidalgo is noted for its locally made ceramics and colonial style furniture. The *ceramicas* are small establishments found throughout the town. Some of them specialize in making cups and mugs, others plates, so if you want to buy a factory-direct set of china you may have to search out a number of different establishments creating the same design.

We enjoyed an interesting meal on a patio restaurant facing the *Plaza Principal*. Carole ordered the Special for the Day—a flaming tableside dish dramatically wheeled tableside by the solicitous Head Waiter. After polishing off her shrimp flamed in tequila, the waiters returned for more pyrotechnics—peaches flamed in brandy followed by a coffee that was also set on fire. Carole said it was wonderful; I may have to get those special pans and *flambé* equipment so the poor girl will enjoy eating again.

San Miguel de Allende

Twenty-five miles south of Dolores Hidalgo is San Miguel de Allende, birthplace of Ignacio Allende who, along with Father Miguel Hidalgo, led Mexico's insurgency in its war of independence. Judging by the large number of Americans that live in San Miguel today, it would appear that Allende's efforts were in vain. President Clinton, I'm told, has offered to give back San Miguel to Mexico if Mexico will return San Antonio. The Americans appear to live very comfortable and active lives in San Miguel and are doing what they can to have a positive impact on environmental, social, economic and cultural aspects. There are brass, tinware, glass, ceramic, silver and weaving workshops in San Miguel. The town has some good stores where you can find these local products as well as crafts produced throughout Mexico. Carole found a string of heavy silver beads, each bead only slightly smaller than a golf ball. Lois, who I am told is an excellent shopper, was at first diffident about bargaining, but tried her hand at shopping on her own. We enjoyed some good meals in various patio restaurants. *El Meson de San Jose*, owned by a German, was a particularly pleasant place, but I believe its owner discovered garlic late in life and is trying to make up for previous omissions.

The San Miguel library association raises money for student scholarships and various other community projects by conducting tours of selected houses. Carole and I have wanted to take the San Miguel Sunday morning house tour since our first visit some years ago, however, each time we have visited San Miguel when the tours were held, something had prevented our participating. While one is free to drive around town and look at houses in San Miguel, Mexican and Spanish architecture usually limits your view past the outside walls and doors. The sponsored tour gives you an opportunity to see what is behind these impressive doors. Solely due to Rod Dittmer's love of "party", Carole and I almost failed to make the tour—again. However, a little worse for wear, Carole and I finally made the 11:00 a.m. start time. I'm glad we did, because it started the "let's build our own house in Mexico" juices flowing.

Apaseo el Alto

About 89 miles east of Guanajuato is the beautiful, colonial and historic city of Queretero, in the State of Queretero. On the way to Queretero is a small town on the eastern edge of the state called Apaseo el Alto. For some time I have wanted to visit and explore this town, because Apaseo el Alto is known for its locally made masks. Apaseo masks are quite different from those made in the rest of Mexico. They are not grotesque with serpents emerging from the mouth nor are they animal masks as is more typical in other parts of Mexico. The ones from Apaseo look like actual people and are described as *realistico,* frankly, almost too real. The masks remind me of those acrylic sculptures of people one is apt to see in modern art museums, only Apaseo masks are made of wood. I had previously stopped at the Guanajuato State Tourist Office to ask about Apaseo el Alto; I was told that Apaseo was not a tourist destination. "But what about the crafts produced there"? The man at the tourist office responded: "Oh sure, they have many crafts, if that's what you are looking for." I didn't tell him that sometimes when I was not busy at the disco or bungee jumping, I liked to see the local *artisania,* and, occasionally I even buy things. There seems to be a bit of a marketing problem here at the State Tourist Office.

The Dittmers, Carole and I left the freeway to explore Apaseo el Alto. At the entrance to the town we found a large shop that sold hand carved furniture and other carved wooden pieces. With San Miguel de Allende only a few miles away, carved statues of the Arch Angel Saint Michael with every fingernail intricately detailed, are a big item here. There were a lot of fine pieces along with some real cornball ones. A carved, life-sized statue of a *campesino* with a bottle of tequila in his hand comes to mind. I asked about the masks of Apaseo el Alto, and the store manager said he had never heard of them. We continued to *El Centro* and found a nice rooftop restaurant overlooking a central plaza. A large church with classic

Greek columns fronted the plaza, but off to another side was a second church, this one painted with riotous colors as bright as any we have seen on any building in Mexico. I suspect that the second church was a people's church built in reaction to the first one, which didn't look very Mexican at all. I asked the restaurant owner about the masks. She thought they still made them and explained that there were over sixty-five shops in town that produced various crafts. Because this was the D*ia de Los Muertos,* D*ay of the Dead, almost all establishments were closed. I would like to return to Apaseo el Alto and continue the exploration of this non-tourist destination.

Queretero

Among the various colonial cities we have visited in Mexico, Queretero, in my view, is the most elegant. The colonial part of the city envelops approximately fifty blocks of the center of town, all of it under some type of historic preservation. Unlike our new hometown of Guanajuato, the streets intersect at right angles, are paved with flat paving stones, curbs are generally a uniform height, sidewalks are wide enough for two or more people, and some streets once adequate for carriages have been closed off from vehicular traffic to make pedestrian promenades. Queretero, being topographically flatter than Guanajuato, was laid out according to Spanish colonial town planning standards and has a great deal of order and form.

Someone in Queretero invented a method of mining that permitted ore removal at great depths. This enormously increased the amount of gold and silver than could be extracted from the mines of Guanajuato and Zacatecas. The inventor of this technique became very wealthy. Judging by the grand architecture that one sees in Queretero, I have a feeling that not all of the mining wealth of places like Guanajuato and Zacatecas ended up in Mexico City or in Spain. I guess you could say, Queretero got the elegant mansions and Guanajuato got the deep shaft.

Facing the central plaza with its traditional bandstand and fountain is *Templo de San Francisco,* completed in 1705. Next to it is the Grand Convent (monastery) of St. Francis Assisi, started in 1540, which now houses the regional museum. The treaty that forced Mexico to cede half of its territory to the U.S. was signed in Queretero in May 1848. The area of land that Mexico lost is larger than Western Europe. In 1916, during another U.S. occupation of Mexico, Queretero served as the nation's capital. Somehow, the good folks of Queretero didn't hold us personally responsible for these incursions, and apparently, we had a fine time there.

Queretero takes special pride in her native heroine, *Dona Josefa Ortiz de Domingues, la Corregadora.* She was the wife of *El Corregador,* the chief magistrate of the city. Dona Josefa informed the insurgents that the Spanish had learned of the plot to revolt. The result was that Father Hidalgo, (remember Hidalgo in Dolores), issued his famous cry for independence. One can see the ornate window of *Dona Josefa's bedroom* in the *Plaza de la Independencia,* where she was locked up during a failed effort to keep her from spilling the *frijoles.* The Plaza is an attractive spot with outdoor restaurants on two sides. It was in Queretero where Emperor Maximilian was captured, tried, and executed by firing squad in 1867 three short years after France's Napoleon III installed him as Emperor of Mexico. Mexico's 1917 Constitution was drafted here, and one can visit the theater where it was written and debated. Queretero's rich historical past has been thoughtfully and tastefully presented.

My tourist guidebook mentioned that in front of the main plaza of the colonial district is the Plaza Hotel with "squeaky clean, comfy rooms—$25 U.S. for a double." They're clean, but I don't know about the squeaky part. Rod Dittmer managed to clog the toilet in his room within fifteen minutes of check-in time. Later he broke off the handle on the purified water jug that was in the hallway. Fortunately, our stay at the Plaza was for only two nights or we might have been arrested for trashing the place. As we were able step out onto a small balcony and look across the Plaza, it was a terrific location, although a noisy one. In the morning, we awoke to the sound of the Mexican army marching down Avenida Juarez just below our balcony. A steady stream of traffic continued all day and night. This section of the street must be the area where local drivers were suppose to test their auto horns to see if they worked. The place was noisy.

When I first suggested the Plaza Hotel, I had hoped for something with a touch of class; perhaps a patio with attractive señoritas serving margaritas as we listened to a superlative Andres Segovia-type guitarist. The Plaza Hotel fell a bit short of my expectations, but as the guidebook informed us, it had a terrific location.

In our wanderings around *El Centro*, we found several lapidaries. Queretero is particularly noted for its opals and fine stones. Carole bought a ring for about twenty dollars with a green stone called chrysophrase. The storeowner explained that chrysophrase was <u>not</u> a semiprecious stone; it was a <u>gemstone.</u> If Carole were to have it reset in a new ring, the jeweler suggested she set it in gold with small diamonds surrounding the stone. I wanted to tell the storeowner it looks fine just the way it is, and we didn't want any flashy diamonds detracting from the chryso-phrase. We wandered into another lapidary and lying on the counter was a book on stones, so I asked about chrysophrase. As the jeweler turned the pages, he told us that chrosophrase is a fine gemstone and should really be set off with dia-monds. I felt it was time to leave opal alley.

To make up for the disappointment of our hotel selection I was hoping we could find a nice bar and have that perfect margarita with or without service by attractive señoritas. We came across an imposing colonial structure that had been made into a hotel. Rooms at la Marquesa start at $150/night, and their price list is denominated in U.S. dollars. (I hope this idea doesn't catch on in Guanajuato.) This was the *Casa de la Marquesa,* and we felt we should check it out by, at least, visiting the bar for a drink. It was a large Spanish colonial building with a heavy Moorish appearance. While in the bar, we asked to take a peek at the menu. There were some fine food choices, and we were surprised at the modest prices offered in such a sumptuous place. So off we went to the dining room for a truly memorable meal. The food and wine were excellent surpassed only by incompa-rable service. The wait staff of three men and two women stood at attention on the far side of the room. I think Rod felt they needed five to serve the four of us because the two women were small. They meticulously and promptly attended to our dining needs with none of that hovering that I hate. It was truly superb ser-vice, much like what we had become accustomed to at Fieler's Restaurant and Neighborhood Bar in Madison, Wisconsin.

On the way out of town we saw Queretero's signature piece, a grand aqueduct consisting of seventy-four massive, graceful arches. Queretero has so much in the way of history and architecture that it deserves further visits. Perhaps next time, we should do it with a guide because I think we missed a lot.

Carlos's First Law of Living in Mexico—*It's Not Wrong, It's Different*

Again and again, it has been demonstrated to me that what I at first think is wrong in Mexico, is not. I am coming to understand that there are reasons for things being the way they are, and if one is going to live in Mexico, one should grasp this important concept. For example, it doesn't do any good to tell a police-man who is removing your license plates with a screwdriver for illegal parking, that this isn't the way they do it in the United States. To do so, would give him the satisfaction of telling you that this is not the United States and removing the plates assures that the owner will appear at the police station and pay the fine.

Last week, I went to get license plates for our car to replace our expiring Wisconsin plates. I drove over to the State traffic police headquarters, a very large and modern—actually modernistic-facility on the edge of town. I say large because it has a parade ground or drill field within the facility although not visible from the outside. One could hear the police drum and bugle corps marching with the police cadets. One of the early conclusions I had assumed about Mexico is that given a tiny amount of authority, the Mexican would wield—to the hilt—whatever power came with the position. I had assumed that this characteristic would loom extra large at the State Police Headquarters and Academy. I was surprised that my initial entry into these walls didn't bear out this generalization. The clerk who sat at the desk was middle-aged and motherly looking. She patiently listened to my request for license plates, rendered in fractured Spanish. I heard her quietly say to another clerk something to the effect that "I don't think he will be able to understand the directions; I'll just walk him over to the correct desk." There were several archways and entryway choices, so I appreciated the personal guide service. She introduced me to an office worker who went over all the papers I had on our car—Wisconsin title, Mexican auto entry permit, drivers license, passport, FM-3, etc. After studying these and reviewing the matter with his supervisor, he informed me that I didn't need state license plates, that my entry permit, which included a hologram windshield sticker, was all that I needed. It was good for a year and could be renewed indefinitely, he added. Well, this was good news in a way, because it would spare me the expense of Mexican plates, which are quite high, and the only fee would be the auto entry permit that I had already paid for. However, I was really trying to establish that our domicile had truly and legally changed and I needed to sever all legal connection with my former State. I will always be very fond of Wisconsin, a state blessed with quality services, but high taxes. But I didn't think we should continue to pay those taxes inasmuch as we don't live in Wisconsin anymore. In my mind, at least, that means that one shouldn't have a Wisconsin driver's license, Wisconsin license plates, or other evidence that you live there if you are going to claim that you have changed your domicile. (I've since learned that an American-titled car is not eligible for Mexico plates until the car is at least 10 years old.)

My next dilemma, one I particularly dreaded, was the prospect of having to take a driver's test on the streets of Guanajuato. While I have successfully managed to park our Ford Windstar van in the *Subteranio*, that's only because I do it when conditions are just right. Imagine for a moment all the traffic on University Avenue in Madison routed through a one-lane, one-way tunnel lacking any straight segments, and where there is one parallel parking lane without marked stalls so that most parking spaces are only large enough for a VW bug. And imagine that every 10th vehicle is a municipal bus that has a schedule to keep; that every 5th vehicle is an owner-operated taxicab whose driver collects the equivalent of $1.50 for a two mile ride and does not receive or expect tips and has to meet payments on his cab with 80% interest rates. Well you get the idea. There is a bit of pressure on anyone parking in the tunnel. Do it fast and get it right the first time. Interestingly enough, the drivers of the big busses are considerate, and perhaps half the taxis drivers are patient, but it is a rare VW driver that abides much delay. I also dreaded a driver's test because of the subtle differences in traffic regulations over those I was accustomed to in Wisconsin. Signs on the highway saying: "Do not leave stones on the pavement" baffled me. I have since learned that as a safety measure, drivers of vehicles with uncertain brakes, when pulling over, would set rocks under the wheels to prevent the vehicle from rolling away. Keep in mind that only 4% of Mexico is flat. The signs remind drivers to remove the rocks before leaving. I now understand the meaning of this regulation, but what about some of the finer points of travel in Mexico, such as: When your car and a big semi-truck each approach a one-lane bridge from opposite directions, who has the right-of-way: the vehicle that gets there first, the one that blinks its lights first, or the largest vehicle capable of inflicting the most damage? As far as I am concerned, it's the big semi-truck. I wanted to ask for a copy of the driving rules and find out what the driver's exam consisted of. What they gave me was a form to fill out.

I almost laughed hysterically when the young officer told me that a driver's exam was not necessary, but what I needed was a physical examination. "Take this form", he said, "to Guanajuato General Hospital for your physical." I was convinced that once again they had it all wrong in Mexico, but off to the hospital I went. The receptionist directed me to a waiting room for physicals. The hospital was light, airy, and quite clean. There were a lot of hand-painted posters urging the use of mother's milk and other health messages. This seemed sensible and was reassuring, but when I caught the signs that identified the different rooms serving the physical exam area, I became worried. The first door was "RAYOS X", and that was O.K.; the next two were dressing rooms, and that was O.K.; but the fourth door was marked: "ENEMAS". No way! I said to myself. When it comes to regulatory requirements, this country must be nuts. I don't need I driver's license that bad. Why do I need a physical exam, why an enema? As I pondered this, my name was called. I was directed into a small room where a nurse removed a needle from a sealed wrapper and pricked my finger to draw some blood. After 20 minutes she handed me a report that gave my blood type,

"O" RH(+). She told me to take the form to the police department. I said, "That's all?" and she said: "That's all."

Eureka! It was then that it came to me: **Carlos's First Law of Living in Mexico:** *It's not wrong; it's different.* Mexico uses blood types on people's driver's licenses to establish a living blood bank. They accepted my Wisconsin driver's license as proof that I could drive the car. It may not be the way we do it in the United States but it makes some sense after all.

As I left the physical exam area of Guanajuato General Hospital I noticed a half dozen baby food jars each filled with yellow fluid. I haven't spent a lot of time in the world of hospitals, but I could surmise that these were urine specimens. Applying **Carlos's First Law of Living in Mexico**, I reasoned that the use of Gerber baby food jars for holding urine specimens, while probably not the way they do it in the U.S., was cost effective and a perfectly reasonable way to do it in Mexico. Why do you need to have expensive special containers for this task? *"It's not wrong; it's different."*

But I also noticed that among the baby food jars was a 3/4-liter mayonnaise jar that looked like it was about two thirds full. The quantity of specimen fluid amazed me a bit, but what gave me real pause was that the Hellmann's label was still on the jar. Now I have considered the possibility that as a means of conducting urine analysis for a small village, or at least an entire family, by having multiple donations, one could run just one test for the whole group. If the results were negative you could conclude with a single test that all was well with the group. Of course, if the results were positive, one would need to have half the group repeat the donation and keep repeating the test until the culprit was discovered. Try as I might to find the logic in this case I had to conclude that this defied logic. And thus: **Carlos's Second Law:** *"But sometimes, it is wrong."*

What I want to do now is work on a unified theory on living in Mexico that will explain exactly when the First Law and when the Second Law are operative.

Season's Greetings to All

With the slow mail service, it will be a miracle if this addition of *Letter from Mexico* reaches you before Christmas. The short-sleeve weather we experience here nearly every day, the lack of snow, and the smattering of palm trees makes it hard to think Christmas. Two years ago when Carole and I lived in Guanajuato for half a year, we learned a bit about a Mexican Christmas from our Spanish language teacher, Veronica. What Veronica described sounded very good to me. Her children each received one gift, something they wanted and that she could afford.

In addition to the religious side of the holiday, they have many parties and good times that usually include the children. Office parties are often held on office time. There are also school parties, neighborhood parties and parties for friends and relatives. We hope to learn more about the holiday customs here in the future.

I read recently that several years ago, it was Sears & Roebuck that first introduced Santa Claus in their Mexico City store. As the Christmas holiday is now very Americanized, he is all over the place. Saint Nick is an irresistible fellow, particularly when he has so many advocates in the business community. At the big department stores in Leon, they are selling natural Christmas trees from the state of Washington, and they were surprisingly fresh to the touch. The stores are decked out with green garlands and other Christmas decorations and American Christmas music is played non-stop. As yet, I have not heard the Spanish language version of the Chipmunks singing Christmas songs, but I know it's out there somewhere as I heard it when we were here two years ago. This is as maddening in Spanish as it is in English.

There are some other indications that Christmas is coming. In our back yard, there is a group of poinsettia plants; at thirteen feet in height, they look more like trees. We have both cream color and red *noche buena,* as they are called here. The red color of these poinsettias is so vivid and is in such a large array that the nearby fifteen-foot stretch of bougainvillea looks pale by comparison. But one sure indication that Christmas is near is the imported Norwegian *lutefisk,* which has recently appeared in the supermarket. Back in Wisconsin, *lutefisk* holiday dinners would be offered by the Norwegian and Swedish Lutheran churches at Christmas time. The dry *lutefisk* would be boiled and served with melted butter. In Mexico, where it is called *baclao,* this fish is prepared with a sauce that has tomatoes, onions, garlic and olive oil and is really quite good. To all our friends, relatives and family we think about you often and wish we could be together at this special time. Hope you all have a very happy holiday. *Feliz Navidad*

Charlie and Carole

4

April 1996

Fiesta at the Monts, The Road to Lake Chapala, The Search for *Terreno,*
Dias de las Flores, The Girls of Guanajuato

Fiesta at the Monts

Our guests were Mike and Maureen Torphy from Madison, Wisconsin. As a way
of getting more acquainted with the people we've met here and to introduce our
guests to a group of Mexican and Anglo friends, we thought it would be fun to
have a party in our back yard. Our friends, Derek and Elisa Young, had visitors
from England so we joined forces on the party. The Youngs furnished the entertainment, and we furnished the drinks and the food. Juaquin, the fellow that
fixed the leaky pipe, and his pretty wife, Beatriz, with help from Chepa, prepared
the goodies. The *jardin* is our small back yard. It is completely walled off from
neighboring properties and has a sheltered barbecue with three built-in charcoal
grills. There are lanterns hanging from the walls so it is nicely set up for an
evening party. Beatriz heated the tortillas on one of the grills for the tacos and
quesadilla. Juaquin, who happens to be a Jehovah's Witness, expertly poured the
drinks. Well, he hadn't always been a Witness. Elisa arranged for our favorite
Estudiantina group to enter the party singing and strumming their guitars and
mandolins.

One of the enjoyable institutions of Guanajuato is the *Estudiantina.* They are
a group of musicians dressed in the garb of medieval Spanish university students
that walk the narrow pedestrian walkways of Guanajuato (*los callejones*) singing
and playing songs—normally followed by a happy crowd of people joining in the
festivities. The group we like best, *La Tuna de Guanajuato Provincial,* sing and
play both Mexican and Spanish songs. I don't actually understand the running
dialog that intersperses the songs, but judging by the laughter from the mainly
youthful crowd, I sense that we're hearing some earthy jokes and comments, all

rendered in good fun. The first time I saw the *Estudiantina*, a burro accompanied the group carrying two small casks of wine served to the crowd that followed. This delightful custom has given way probably from complaints from people living on the *callejones* and, no doubt, their concern for certain sanitary conditions. At any rate, my first siting of the *Estudiatina* found them singing their way to the famous *Callejon del Beso*—a callejón narrow enough so that two lovers of Guanajuato legend could kiss each other from facing balconies without leaving their homes; they were defying the orders of the girls father, a wealthy Spanish mine owner. Legend has it that dad killed his daughter for disobeying his orders to stay away from her lover, Carlos. Parental tough love was very strict, obviously. Today, the cask-toting burros have been replaced with a *porrón*, a narrow-necked, ceramic pitcher filled with wine. Purchasing your refreshment supports the cost of the *Estudiantina*. The porrón allows you to pour a thin stream of wine directly into your mouth without your lips touching the vessel, but for the novice, be prepared to get a face-full if you don't do it just right. The leader of the group explains, with mock seriousness, that they have spared no expense in providing a full quart (more like five ounces) of the finest imported wine from France (more like Mogan David) and that the cost of the wine, including the *porrón*, is not fifty pesos as you would expect for quality such as this, but a mere twenty pesos, or about $2.00.

Well, the folks at our party sang and danced with this group of musicians late into the night; we all had a great time!

The Road to Lake Chapala

While vacationing in Guanajuato, the Torphy's opted for some beach time in Puerto Vallarta. So off we went. While it might be possible to drive from Guanajuato straight through to Puerto Vallarta in one long day of driving, it makes more sense to break up the trip into two segments. Approximately half way to Vallarta is Guadalajara, and twenty miles southeast of it is Lake Chapala. The lake is sixty miles long and has a string of small towns and villages along its shores. Our destination for our first night's rest was one of these villages, Ajijic, pronounced Ah-he-heek. (Note the four consecutive dots in the name. Can there be any other place name in the world with this letter construction?) To reach Ajijic from Guanajuato, in the most direct fashion, requires driving on an ever-changing series of Mexican primary and secondary roads. The easier alternative is to take the very fine, although overpriced, toll road to Guadalajara that runs west from Guanajuato. The autopista, however, directs one into the heart of the

Guadalajara metropolis connecting with another expressway to Lake Chapala that actually backtracks in a southeast direction.

At my urging, we started with the most direct route option, the one that requires several changes of questionable roads. We got lost almost immediately and voted four to zero to switch over to the freeway to Guadalajara. But rather than driving all the way into the city, why not take a short cut and save about twenty miles of travel? The highway map indicated that the cut-off was a paved road, so while it might not be as high speed as the toll road, it still should save some time. The road was paved all right, but the paving was cobblestone. The area we were rumbling through was not backwoods but, more accurately, might be termed back-cactus, and not very well marked. We found ourselves losing the "trail" several times. At one point, I saw two people just ahead busily doing something on the left side of the road. I thought this would provide an opportunity to ask if this were the road to El Salto, the next town on the map. As I pulled up, to my astonishment, I saw a girl who looked to be about fourteen years old wielding a pick ax on the cobblestones of the road. With her was a boy of about ten holding a shovel. Both looked very somber with their task. The girl kept digging, but the boy stopped and said something to me in Spanish that I didn't understand. I have since figured out that what he was saying was, "Can you help us?"

Often when I am about to render a question in Spanish, I try to formulate the question in advance and silently practice saying the phrase. In this instance, I didn't really listen to the boy or ask him to repeat what he was saying. Instead, I simply blurted out my question: "Was this the road to El Salto?" The boy responded in the affirmative, so I started to drive off. I noticed, however, that the cobblestones had been cleared from the roadway in a neat rectangle measuring about three by six feet. Parked adjacent to this rectangle was an old pickup truck with an opened umbrella inside screening the passenger's side of the seat from the hot sun. It looked like someone was slumped against the umbrella that pressed the side window of the truck. As I drove off, it dawned on me that the children were burying someone, most likely a parent. Could I have helped? Probably not in any significant way. We've learned that we shouldn't get involved in what we don't understand, but perhaps a few pesos, a bottle of water passed out the window, or a kind word would have gone a long way in a situation like this.

The Search for *Terreno*

Our house on Camino Antigua is nice in many ways, but it does have some limitations and aggravations. In a town where there are many fine vistas, our house is tucked in a valley bottom among old haciendas—lovely, but offering none of the great panoramic views afforded by the mountainous topography more typical of Guanajuato. At times, especially during the dry, hotter season, the river goes anaerobic on us—it smells. Most troublesome is the dust from Camino Antigua. And, for a city with a consistently pleasant climate, it is disappointing that our house lacks good cross ventilation. Carole and I think we can find something better, so we've started to check out the local real estate market.

We've visited some spectacular houses almost within our financial means, but on closer examination, we found many were lacking. It seems in Guanajuato, houses of good quality generally tend to be huge and include features we don't need or want. I mean, do you think Carole and I will ever start playing handball in our own private handball court or take up rifle shooting in our own lower level shooting gallery? One place we were serious about had a spectacular view of the city, marble floors, and a kidney shaped swimming pool large enough to include a footbridge across its narrow end. During the 9-month dry season in Guanajuato, water supply is precious. A pool this size would be unconscionable and probably unfillable. This house also had a separate room with a steam bath but didn't have a place where I could set up a small workshop, which, I believe, is a must. It seems obvious to me that people here with a little bit of money can have whatever they want in a house. Trouble is, their whims don't quite match our dreams.

About the time we started to realize the difficulty of finding the kind of house we were looking for, we had some discussions with a couple of architects. One of them explained that he could build us a house at a construction cost of 900 pesos per square meter, about $11.15 per square foot. (Now this is a house without *detales,* details; in other words, pretty plain.) If this were true, a house the size of our place in Madison, not including the basement or garage, would cost $25,700 to build here. Sounds just right, so we have spent the last several months looking for a suitable building site. Finding suitable *terreno* for a house has proven difficult. Building sites are scarce, and as such, not cheap.

But, after a lot of searching, we finally found some property in an actual subdivision. It has a great view, a paved road, streetlights and all the utility services. Of course, there is a bit of paper work connected with this purchase, and it may be several days before we close the deal—even if everything goes well.

As we conducted our search for *terreno*, we happened to come across another house for rent on the *Panoramica.* Recognizing that it would be some time before we could move into our newly built house, we thought we could improve our living during construction time and be closer to the project. Our new rented home has a view of *Las Embajadoras*, "The Lady Ambassadors", a small park and public market that forms an attractive cityscape.

This house has a large living/dining room with fireplace and a balcony, a moderate sized kitchen with pantry, a TV sitting room with a small balcony, and three bedrooms. The master bedroom has its own balcony and a clothes closet that connects to a master bath. The guest bedroom has its own bathroom. There is a small maid's room with a bathroom, and there is a half bath on the main floor. There is a walled garden area and a laundry area (*servicio*). I intend to use the maid's room for a small workshop.

Dias de las Flores

As far as I know, Guanajuato is the only town in Mexico that celebrates a Day of the Flowers as a prelude to Palm Sunday. Vendors bring in an enormous quantity of fresh flowers and attractive flowers made from colored paper, painted burlap and cornhusks. They also have an amazing array of confetti dispensers made from brightly painted eggs that have been emptied of their contents. The idea is to make the confetti-filled eggshell look like something else. Ice cream cones are the most common form, but one also sees pigs, clowns and a dazzling variety of items, all artfully made from eggshells. They use these to bop someone on the head spraying them with very fine confetti.

On the Thursday before Palm Sunday, the city closes off a section of Guanajuato's main street, Avenida Juarez, to accommodate the crowds and vendors. At 11 P.M., dancing starts in the street and adjacent plaza. We didn't check this out, but I was told that dancing continues throughout the night with breakfast offered the next morning at nearby restaurants. We did, however, return for breakfast the next morning at the second floor restaurant of the Hotel San Diego. The restaurant overlooks the *Jardin Union* and *Avenida Juarez* and is probably the best spot in town to view the festivities. Getting to the hotel involved our walking through a sea of humanity. It seemed like half of the crowd was going in an opposite direction from our party. The ladies carried bouquets of flowers, and the children were bopping each other with the confetti cones. As I pressed my way through the crowd, I encountered Vincente Fox, Governor of the State of Guanajuato, coming the other way. "*Buenos dias,*" he said to me; "*Buenos dias*", I replied. Governor Fox stands about six foot three and looks like a movie star. Many people say that he will be the next president of Mexico. He patted me on the shoulder—I was thankful that it was not on top of my head. Having established such close contact with him, I wanted to offer him some pointers on state planning, but was pushed on by folks behind me. This encounter gives a new meaning to the notion of pressing the flesh so popular with political types.

The Girls of Guanajuato

No travel book on Mexico is complete without the inclusion of visiting Guanajuato. One can learn about Guanajuato's history, its legends, architecture, vistas and points of interest. Oddly enough, however, none of the writers of these travel books has documented, or even mentioned, what I believe is one of Guanajuato's outstanding attractions: the girls and young women of this colonial gem. I've been told that the first travel writers that visited this city were a husband and wife team. After arriving here and observing the scene the husband said to his wife, "OK, honey, you cover the museums and restaurants; I'll check out the hotels and the girls." No one knows what happened to this travel writer, but the girls have not been included in travel literature since. At least this is one explanation.

Let me be the first to point out that there is a disproportionate number of beautiful women here. Something unusual seems to have happened in this semi-remote section of the world because the normal bell curve distribution of female beauty is definitely skewed to the good-looking side. (OK, I know that some of you may be wondering what about the boys and young men. What do they look like, and why am I limiting this report to feminine beauty? Listen up my friends. Explaining to my wife, Carole, why I am writing about the girls and young women of Guanajuato is probably as much as my skills at explaining things can hope to accomplish. Including boys in this report is definitely out of the question. Oh, and let me further explain that while I very much admire the aqueducts and the pyramids of Mexico, that doesn't mean I intend to bring one home with me. With that explanation, I'd like to get back to the girls of Guanajuato. Hey. Who wouldn't?)

My research into this pulchritudinous abnormality extant in Guanajuato reveals the following (I'm trying to be as scientific as I can.) First, while not all of the girls and young women in this town are beautiful, there are more beautiful females than can be explained by any normal distribution factor. Second, the beauties can be classified into three groups. At the very top, are the "Drop Dead Beauties." These women are truly exquisite but rarely observed by tourists, because visitors here are too busy looking at the historic buildings or seeking out a clean restroom. In the second group, are the "Knockouts." One can view them all over the place. And then there are a lot of really pretty girls.

Of course the big question is **WHY**? Why so many good-looking girls and young women? (Ford Foundation people, where are you when I really need a research grant?) My preliminary analysis reveals several possibilities. Let me discuss these.

• Virtually all of the small children in Guanajuato are as cute as can be. Little girls look like little angels. With such an overwhelming percentage of lovely children it is probably unavoidable that many little girls reach womanhood looking absolutely smashing.

• So many of the people living here have at least some percentage of indigenous blood. Thus, they are favored with high cheekbones, the same facial characteristic that has catapulted so many Nordic women onto the Hollywood screen.

• The Guanajuato *callejones*, those narrow and unusually steep walkways, some of which turn into steps because the grades are so steep, provide the only access to many of the houses in the city. Walking these steep grades and steps on a daily basis would render a gal with legs that started out looking like sausages into a gal with Lana Turner gams. (Please note how I date myself.)

• It is a statistical fact that the average age of the Mexican people is nineteen years. Hey, you and I probably weren't so bad looking when we were nineteen? Add to this fact that in a city of 83,000 people, Guanajuato has a state university with 32,000 students, maybe half of whom are female. Not surprising that you can expect a lot of pretty young faces.

• Another factor is that many women here, especially those with slender waists, seem to be afflicted with a rare malady that requires fresh air on their navels. I fear that without cool air on their belly buttons, they shrivel up and die—so exposed mid-drifts in Guanajuato are de rigueur, even in winter.

• Unlike their sisters who reside at lower elevations and are under considerable atmospheric pressure, the high altitude of Guanajuato allows a healthy expansion of female boobs, thus permitting their beauty to fully peak.

There are lots of other possible explanations. I recently read that the traditional Mexican diet of corn tortillas, beans, rice, and chili peppers is very healthy. I can't remember if it's vitamins, enzymes, or what; but I do recall that one of the several benefits of this diet is beautiful, white teeth. When a Guanajuato beauty smiles at you, all you can do is stand there and grin, and kick yourself for not having enrolled in one of those total immersion Spanish courses that you promised yourself you would begin.

For those of you who doubt my observations, come to Guanajuato and check it out for yourself. In the meantime, I'll keep you posted on my continuing research.

5

June 1996

Montemayors Reach New Heights, Lot Purchased, Preliminary Plans Completed

Montemayors Reach New Heights

The new house we were renting on the *Panaoramica* has turned out to be a real joy for us. Guanajuato was built on the slopes of a meandering canyon. Surrounding the city is a 22-mile *Panoramica* road overlooking and spanning the central city. From one side of the *Panoramica* to the other is less than a mile wide. From our balcony you can watch the sunrise over the mountains on the opposite side of the canyon with a splendid view of the city below. The guidebooks give an altitude in Guanajuato of about 6,800 feet; however, from our home on the Panoramica, we are high enough that we're able to watch flocks of birds swirling below us. To me the view is like looking down on a miniature town. One can see the entrance to a new tunnel, one of Guanajuato's municipal markets, houses compactly arrayed on the sides of the canyon, and boxy looking busses straining up the steep grades. At night, Guanajuato is aglow with thousands of lights. It is enchanting.

The only downside may be the winds. Surrounded as we are by mountains, there have been many nights, and a few days, during which the winds have picked up to a mighty howl. This seems to be a function of the immediate topography and the fact that this has been a windier [than normal] spring. I think our house may be in a notch, although it is not that obvious to us for the house below us only a hundred feet away has a clothesline outside, and for whatever reason, while we are being beaten with horrendous winds, the hanging clothes only gently sway. It seems a bit strange to experience these high winds, particularly with no clouds in sight. Where are they coming from? May, which averages 70.5 degrees, is the warmest month in Guanajuato. The air temperature can reach the mid- to high-80's, but living as we do in a mighty vortex of rushing air, we haven't suffered from a lack of air conditioning.

Lot Purchased, Preliminary Plans Completed

After searching many *terrenos*, we finally found something our architect, Efren Fonseca, and we, agreed would be suitable for our permanent home. There are many difficulties in finding a building site in Guanajuato. At least half of the houses and lots are not accessible by car. Many which do have auto access lack water, electricity, sewerage, or phone service. Many that have the necessary services have incompatible surrounding uses or look down on what are called *casas populares*—houses of the people. A lot of good can be said of these owner-built houses, but attractiveness is generally not their strong point. Of the few lots that have an access road, a view, and services, half of them slope down from the road. Because lots are generally steep and narrow, it is quite typical for a house to be three stories with a garage built on top at street level. This is not suitable for us because of the difficulty Carole would have in carrying me to bed when I get really old.

What we finally found, and bought, was land that slopes up from a paved cobblestone street. It has all the services and even street trees and streetlights. The best feature of all is the beautiful view of the city below us where we can see two historic aqueducts and many old churches illuminated at night. We've explained to our architect that we want to capitalize on this view. Also important for us is that we don't have to climb any more steps than absolutely necessary. The lot is too steep for a driveway going straight to the house, so we've bought two lots giving us the room for a U-curved drive to get our car closer to the house.

Carole and I have prepared a schedule of what is needed and wanted in our house. The house is to be, essentially, on one level, with the exception of a two-car garage and workshop that can be below the house. We also felt that because the weather here is so consistently pleasant, we would like to be able to step out onto a *terraza*, covered porch, from the main living quarters and, too, from the bedrooms into a garden. We didn't say what we wanted the house to look like other than that we wanted the house to look *muy Mexicana*. We are anxious to get started.

We are pleased with the plans and elevations that the architect has prepared for us. While Guanajuato does not have zoning that controls the use of land, it does has strict architectural design controls on buildings within the historic zone. One cannot change the outside appearance of an existing building, and for buildings that face the *zona historica,* as ours does, they must conform to design that is in the style of Guanajuato. One of the things we admire about Mexican houses is the sloped tiled roof; we want one on our house. We also want *boveda* ceilings, which are beautiful brick domed ceilings that are said to have originated in Catalonia, Spain and are a specialty of craftsman here in Guanajuato. The odd thing is that in an area such as ours, if you have internal *boveda* ceilings, the dome configuration cannot be visible from the outside. Consequently, a balustrade has to be built to screen off the *bovedas,* making the house appear taller than we would have preferred but, all in all, we are pleased with the design.

6

September 1996

Visit to the US, Returning Home to Guanajuato, Progress on New House, Picking up the Pieces

Visit to the US

Although we had planned to depart Guanajuato at daybreak on Sunday, July 7, we both overslept. Juaquin and his wife Beatriz were to come over to see us off and take care of our house during our absence. Too polite to pound on the door instead of just touching on the doorbell, they returned home and let us sleep. We didn't get on the road until 8:30 that morning. Fortunately, truck traffic in Mexico is light on Sundays, and we reached the border at Laredo, Texas early that evening in spite of our late start. This is a 572-mile trip. A fair amount of it was on freeways called *autopistas*. Laredo is a bustling border town that, on each occasion of our passage, has greeted us with temperatures in the 100's. Our plan was to stay overnight in a motel in the Laredo area so that we could buy car insurance for our trip to the U.S. The only lodging requirement that we had was that the room had to have air conditioning, and because we were arriving late and checking out early, we were not looking for anything fancy. We drove up and down the streets of Laredo singing you know what song until we found a place called the Aztec Motel. The reception area did not have air conditioning but had a couple of fans going. I thought it would be prudent to ask about their system of climate control in the motel rooms. Now I have no idea if the Aztec is a part of the Helmsley Hotel chain, but I am sure that Leona never checked this place out. The desk clerk at the Aztec had a peculiar way of answering questions. When I asked if they had air conditioning in the rooms, he answered by asking if we had air conditioning where we lived. I said no, because it stays pretty cool in the warm season and we don't need it. This apparently was the wrong response, because he then asked if I thought he was breaking the law. I inferred from this that Laredo, or perhaps Texas, requires air conditioning in all public accommodations. As I had no way of determining any criminal proclivities on his part, and evasiveness is probably not a crime, I responded, "No, I didn't think he was the sort of person who would break the law." Bingo, that must have been the correct answer because he showed us our room.

As hot as it was in Laredo that night, it was hard to imagine that we would be cold again or, for that matter, ever cool off. However, the air conditioner in our room at the Aztec diabolically seemed to lack any setting between "MAX" and "BLOW HOT AIR ON BODY." We alternated from freezing to boiling. After a grueling day driving through Mexico, my night at the Aztec was spent getting up to fine-tune the system by turning the cooling unit on and off.

I am not going to relate events of the thirty-one marvelous days we had visiting family and friends in the U.S. and the delightful stay we had in the lakeside condo of my former associate, Bill Lane. After all, this is supposed to be a letter from Mexico. The United States, and especially Wisconsin, looked beautiful. I have never seen an August in Madison where everything looked so green. Cities, towns and countryside were exceptionally neat and orderly. Was this the same U.S. we left behind?

Returning Home to Guanajuato

We had purchased a few hundred dollars worth of items in the U.S. and had some concern about what we were required to declare at the border and whether we would have to pay duty on our purchases. Carole and I removed the tags on all the clothes we purchased so they could mingle with the clothes we had when we started our trip. I removed the packaging from various items purchased for our new house in Guanajuato. In the back of our van I have a big plastic box. I threw as much as I could in the box placing rolls of toilet paper, wire coat hangers, a thermos jug, and other uninteresting things on the top. Everything would be visible for Mexican Customs to see, but I didn't think I had to include the slick American packaging that virtually screams out, "Look at me, look at me, I'm brand new and will be sold without the burden of duties." After we crossed the International Bridge, we pulled over at Customs and opened the van. They asked if we had anything to declare. I answered only personal items and things for our house. The customs agent said, "What's that?" pointing to three electric baseboard heaters that remained in their attractive packages and were too large to throw in the bin. "Those are for our house," I explained. "O.K.," he said. All of this took a minute. But then he asked us why we didn't have a new "*steeker*" for the car. I was prepared for that and brought out a copy of a letter from the Mexican Treasury Department given to me by the American Consul in San Miguel. The folks at the Consulate explained that the letter said that in accordance with section such and such of the Federal Laws of the Republic of Mexico that as long as our FM-3 permit was up-to-date that we could keep our American car in Mexico. The pertinent paragraph was highlighted in yellow Day-Glo. After consulting with other agents we were waived through. We knew, of course, that another check was due at kilometer 25. Upon arriving there, we repeated the same procedure regarding our purchases. No problem. However, the letter from Treasury didn't convince them regarding our permission to keep our car without purchasing a hologram sticker allowing us to bring a car into Mexico. I kept referring to the highlighted paragraph, and the agent asked if I could read Spanish. I told him I could read a little but not this legal stuff, which is truly formidable. He smiled just a bit and said I should refer to the preceding paragraph, and that's why they couldn't let us go on. Apparently one paragraph says you can bring your car in and another says you can't unless you buy the *steeker*. After our return to Guanajuato I checked with the American Consul and was told that the Customs agent had been wrong; the letter should have been accepted. While this is reassuring I'm not sure how one goes about informing Mexican Customs that the *Consulado de los Estados Unidos* said they didn't properly understand the laws of the their own country. After half an hour spent discussing this difference, I asked them what they thought we should do. They told me to return to the Customs Office in Nuevo Laredo to buy a new *"steeker."* "How much?" "Eleven dollars." Oh, God, is that all! Sometimes you can press a point mindlessly. **(Edited Note: In 2002, The Mexican government clarified this matter. Once issued, it is no longer necessary to renew an American car's Mexican registration with each crossing, but it seems that the ruling is not understood at all points and is subject to local interpretation.)**

I must say that the several agents we spoke with were polite, but firm, and I had no sense that anyone was looking for payola. In spite of Mexico's reputation for *mordida*, the bite or bribe, I had the feeling that an offer would have been an insult—not to mention illegal. In eighteen months of living in Mexico we have never offered, paid, or been solicited for a bribe. I regret to say that the only people who have suggested that we offer a bribe have been fellow Americans. I know that Mexico has a bad reputation for this sort of thing. I expect that someone is going to suggest we submit our eighteen-month claim for graft-free living to Guinness to see if we have set a world record.

When we arrived at our home in Guanajuato everything was in beautiful order thanks to Chepa, Juaquin, Beatriz and especially to Eliza Young, who managed our checking account, paid our utility bills, and the bills for our house construction. I have a high-low thermometer at our house and noted that during the four weeks of our trip, the maximum temperature had been 81, the low 67. Ah, *la clima templada*. It was nice to be back.

Progress on New House

We were quite amazed at how much had been completed on our new place while we were gone. My first visit to the site surprised me. There must have been twenty-four workers pouring concrete, cutting stone, laying brick and stone, bending wire around reinforcing rods used in the concrete columns, and digging ground with pick axes and shovels for the foundations and driveway. All of the work is being done with hand tools with the exception of two air hammers brought in to chisel away part of the rocky slope. Our lot, which is about 115 feet deep, has an elevation of 35 feet from the lowest front corner to the highest rear corner. The architect achieved something of a small miracle in house design. Considering the slope of the lot and our desire to have a one-level home, he accomplished our wishes with a minimum of earth moving. It's not that the house is tilted; he did it by including a step or two between various rooms, so that the house gently climbs up the hillside in a few easy steps. The excavated part accommodates part of the garage and my workshop. I learned from Sr. Fonseca that the project amounted to 25 cubic meters of jackhammer excavation. The ceiling over the garage and workshop is being made of reinforced concrete, *concreto armado*. This was something we asked the architect to include so that we would have a place to go in the event of earthquake tremors. Local people, including architects and engineers, have told us that while many parts of Mexico are earthquake prone, sometimes disastrously so; Guanajuato is not. In hundreds of years, the city has not suffered any earthquake damage. One can observe very old, spindly-looking church steeples here that have withstood the test of time. We believe, however, that *concreto armado* is a prudent addition to our house. If the earth starts to rumble, we know we have a safe place.

Picking up the Pieces

A fun part of our building project is selecting some of the pieces that go into construction of the house. Our architect told us we shouldn't delay too much in picking out the kind of floor tiles and doors we wanted, because the factories and workshops need time to make them for us. A few days ago, Efren and I drove to San Felipe, a town of about 20,000 people in the northern part of the State. San Felipe lies in the base center of a flat fertile valley with low mountains on each side. One of San Felipe's industries is a clay tile factory. Efren explained that the tiles are made by hand, well not exactly by hand. The clay is mixed by workmen in bare feet mashing the clay mixture in a fashion we associate with Italian grape harvests, wine making, and films with Sophia Loren. The clay is then pressed by hand into molds that are kiln-fired. The tiles all have a pinkish clay color, not exactly what Carole and I had envisioned for our floors, but the workshop owner showed us the tile floor in his office and explained that the deep reddish-brown color comes from applying linseed oil every six months. No polishing or scrubbing is necessary. Just dry mop and renew the oil twice a year.

Selecting the shape and size of tile was not easy. It's not as if they had a display room with patterns laid out for customers to consider. We passed the kilns to an area where the finished tiles were stacked and warehoused. A couple of workmen started laying out squares, rectangles, hexagons, crescents, parallelepipeds, in numerous sizes ranging from three inches to about fourteen and in combinations so that we could see the effect. Some of the arrangements looked so appealing that I changed my mind about staying with simple squares. Efren and I placed a tentative order for 310 square meters, enough to tile the entire house, terrazas and outdoor patios. This adds up to 370 square yards. At $2.95 per square yard, the total price of $1,092 for all our floors seemed quite reasonable. We brought samples back for Carole to see. Because of some concerns she had, we made some changes and phoned the revisions in.

On our return from San Felipe, Efren and I stopped at Dolores Hidalgo, a city that has several shops that sell antique house parts. At one place we found a heavy colonial door about 42 inches wide and four inches thick for the front door to the wall of our house. At this shop they sell both colonial pieces as well as some old items. Colonial doesn't mean colonial style; it means that it was from the colonial period, that is, before Mexico's independence from Spain. This door had rows of wrought iron bossed nail heads. There must be a name for these but they are essentially nails with escutcheons of a scalloped design, each about one and half inches in diameter. These are not the beautiful bronze nail heads one sees on some Spanish colonial mansions in Guanajuato and Queretero, but all the same, very impressive. I asked the sales clerk if she knew the provenance of this door. She shook her head no. Well, I think I can tell you something about the family that had this door. I think they were very lucky people and while they may have not lived elegantly, I bet they lived quite well. I mean there weren't any bullet holes, or things like that in that door.

Last Thursday, Carole and I took off for Patzquaro, about 145 miles away, which is just south of us in the State of Michoacan. Patzcuaro, along with Guanajuato, is one of Mexico's colonial gems and is an interesting place to visit. We found a fine old hotel across from the basilica that turned out to be a pleasant place to stay. Our room faced the church and opened onto a patio courtyard. It was cool at night but not quite cold enough to light the wood in the fireplace in our room; after all, it was still August. The area in and around Patzcuaro is famous for its crafts. Painted clay figures, copper ware, guitars, wool weaving, lacquer ware, and woodcarvings, are some things produced in this area. The purpose of our trip was to purchase carved doors for our house. The doors we saw at the workshop that Efren suggested we visit were intricate, of deep relief and beautiful. We started with the idea of selecting a design for the front door and another plainer design for all the interior doors. We got carried away and selected an array of different designs for the various rooms. The Spanish adjective describing doors carved like this is *elaborado,* which describes our doors to a "T".

Scottish Distillery's Marketing Error Proves Bonanza for Mont's

Items imported into Mexico are usually expensive while locally produced items are often a bargain. For example, one can buy a bottle of Grande Marnier liquor made in Mexico under license from Marnier Lapostelle, Paris for $9.31. That is less than half the price of Grande Marnier imported from France. We don't actually drink Marnier, we use it for cooking and medicinal purposes only. I found a recipe in Diana Kennedy's *Art of Mexican Cooking*: Mangos Flambé in Grand Marnier and tequila. A very luscious desert.

Over the years Carole and I have enjoyed drinking dry Rob Roy's, which is Scotch whisky with a touch of dry vermouth. Mexico makes many things, but it doesn't make Scotch whisky. We had to wonder when we moved here if we had to give up our Rob Roy's because of the high price of the main ingredient. Recently, I found a brand of scotch whiskey, unfamiliar to me, at the big supermarket here. It's called The Clansman and sells for $5.20 for .75 liters. It's distilled and bottled in Scotland and doesn't taste bad. I can't prove this, but I have a theory that they tried to market The Clansman in the U.S. It probably lacked the right cachet to appeal to American drinkers although they may have sold a few bottles in places where they wear white robes and hoods. Stuck with thousands of bottles of The Clansman, I figured they shipped the stuff off to Mexico where the people would look at the label and think clansmen are just knobby-kneed Gringos that wear funny clothes.

7

November 1996

House Construction on Schedule, Monts Put Big Dent in Guanajuato Unemployment, A Little Bit More About the House We're Building, Four Hundred Year Family Reunion

House Construction on Schedule

We were warned that if we were going to build a house in Guanajuato we should be prepared for three things to happen: first, we would encounter many problems; second, the project would not be completed on time (expect a year or two instead of the six months we were told); and, third, costs would be about double the original estimate.

What we have found is that the architect and the *maestros* resolve problems. The *maestros* are the foremen or master craftsmen that run the job at the direction of the architect. One day, I happened to mention to *Maestro, Don Juan,* that there didn't seem to be any problems with this construction job. He explained to me this was because there was a hierarchy in a project such as this. At the very top is *El Patron.* (I have to interrupt here for a moment to explain that the English equivalents of some of these Spanish words, such as *patrón* and *peón,* embarrass me because they sound so, so…feudal. As a good Democrat, I have trouble thinking of myself as a Patrón. Patron, as the English dictionary defines it, is a "patron saint, protector, benefactor, a person, usually wealthy and influential, who sponsors and supports some person or activity." It also bothers me that the people who do the unskilled, heavy work, are called peons. Where is the dignity in that? I'm not suggesting we give them fancy business cards, but don't they deserve a better title than **peon**?) But I digress. Juan went on to explain that if a problem comes up and the peons can't solve it, it moves up to the skilled workers, such as the masons, stonecutters or carpenters. If they can't handle it, it moves up to the *maestros,* such as himself, then to the *arquitecto,* and finally to *el Patrón.* Because of this hierarchy, he explained, there shouldn't be any problems for *el Patrón.* As Oliver Hardy use to say to Stan Laurel, "So far so good, Stanley." I know there is sufficient opportunity for problems to emerge, but so far the system seems to work; we have not had any problems. As for construction delays, the project, if anything, is slightly ahead of schedule. Our architect, Efren Fonseca, has kept his estimated completion by the beginning of December. We are planning on moving by the end of the year.

Cost of the project is up from what we originally expected. This is due more to changes and additions rather than the work costing more than originally estimated. We'll have to see how this turns out.

Monts Put Big Dent in Guanajuato Unemployment

We receive CNN and American TV network news on our digital satellite TV. We have heard President Clinton mention, once or twice (a day) that his administration created ten and a half million new jobs in four years. I think that's terrific, but what about us? We created forty-five new jobs in a couple of months, and we did it with our own money. I was astonished to learn from Efren that our construction project, which is only a three-bedroom house, had, at its peak employment, forty-five workers. Some of these are employees of sub-contractors, and the rest are our workers. I visit the site every day and it amazes me how many people are working on this job, although I never actually counted them. I can see how hard they work, and it gives me a certain satisfaction in seeing all this industry directed at completing our future home. But at other times I worry; who the heck is paying for all of this?

On one occasion, I arrived near the end of the lunch break and it looked like that battlefield scene in the movie, "Patton." Remember that unforgettable scene where bodies and equipment are laying all over the battlefield, and on the day after the great battle, Patton says, "God help me, but I do love it." Well, our building site reminds me of that scene. Bodies are sprawled all over the hillside along with pickaxes, sledgehammers and shovels. A few fires are still smoldering where the workers have cooked their tortillas and beans. The workers in repose look like they will never rise again. It's like the Patton movie except here, all the casualties appeared to have taken place in the shade. Soon however, the men get up and the work goes on. God help me, but I do love it.

One day, Efren told us that the men had completed a certain demanding and difficult stage in the construction. It would be a nice thing if we put on a feed for them. We purchased tortillas, thin Mexican style beefsteaks, an industrial size can of Jalapeno chili peppers and Coca Cola, the national drink of Mexico. The men cooked the meat on steel drum tops over open wood fires. Carole baked a batch of potatoes, which I took to the site along with a kilo of butter for the worker's repast. Efren later told me that the workers said I was *un buen patrón.* I find myself getting more accustomed to the *patrón* role as time passes.

From the beginning of the project, I vowed to avoid interfering in the work. I told Efren that I intended to visit the site every day and watch what was going on. If I saw something that looked wrong to me, I would save my comments for him alone, as he was the one in charge. Efren appreciated this a lot, and while he speaks very little English, he said he and I, as architect and client, were the "Dream Team."

There were, however, a few things that did not seem quite right to me. For example, one day I saw two—count them—two workers straightening out bent nails with a hammer so as not to waste the nails. Because the house is of masonry construction, nails are pounded into the walls to run lines as a guide for keeping the rows of bricks level. Of course, pounding nails into cement walls produces a lot of bent nails, but it seems a waste of worker's time to straighten them out for re-use. Another thing I noticed was that the tools they were using were home-made and quite rudimentary, although to a hardware freak like me, it seemed quite ingenious how they were able to make them. Efren explained to me that under Mexican labor law, workers who furnish their own tools receive a 3 percent pay increment. Many of these tools are made of iron reinforcing rods that have been tempered over fire. I saw a cleverly crafted hacksaw made of a piece of iron reinforcing rod. There were chisels of various sizes, and special tools designed for bending reinforcing rods and wires into cage like forms for reinforcing poured concrete. The wooden handles for the various hammers and sledges were fashioned with a machete knife from branches of a tree cut down on the site.

A project such as this requires a *velador* (watchman), who remains at the site after the workmen have left for the day. Our *velador* is a fellow nicknamed Chava. When Efren was hiring workers for this job, Chava successfully pleaded with him to hire him both as a velador and as a construction worker. This means that Chava is here twenty-four hours a day, seven days a week, either working or guarding the building site. While this is not exactly proper, it is something Chava wanted very much. It seems that he and his wife were having some domestic problems and he lacked a place to live. The construction shack, while not exactly the Hotel Parador San Javier, would be suitable although a bit snug. Chava's cot is underneath a shelf that holds hammers and other tools. I have been assured on a number of occasions that Guanajuato does not share Mexico City's proclivity for seismicity, so I guess it's O.K.

I became acquainted with Chava during my late afternoon visits and have enjoyed chatting with him. One day, he and I were looking at the stream that runs through an arroyo across the street from our property. A small aqueduct of some antiquity spans this river with a single graceful arch. It's a feature I have admired on many previous visits. I could never understand, however, why this aqueduct crossed over a river, particularly when it doesn't seem to go anywhere. I asked Chava why anyone would build an aqueduct that way and he responded, "*puro lujo*," which means "pure extravagance." From Chava's perspective, rich people do things like that simply because they have so much money. There is probably a bit more logic behind this early public works project although I haven't discovered it yet.

Occasionally I have stopped at the site while bringing a case of beer back to our house. Chava and I would chat, have a beer together, and watch the sun set over the mountains. On one such occasion, the sun set exactly in line with the Cristo Rey monument. This is an enormous statue of Christ that sits on a peak about ten miles away. A video of this sunset taken from our terazza exactly on the one day of the year that produces this alignment would make one great commercial for the Catholic Church. (Pass this on if you like.) Once, I met Chava's wife and his little girl who had come to visit him. The three of us enjoyed a bottle of beer together. Often when I arrive, Chava is standing high atop the roof with his machete in hand. I don't know if this is his usual deployment or if this high degree of readiness is enacted when he sees my car coming. Chava has a dog, Pancho, who stays with him. This has caused some consternation at the work site, because three other workers are also named Pancho. The canine, Pancho, looks like he is part Malamute. He is very gentle and his demeanor doesn't seem to fit the role of watchdog. I don't think he was really cut out for this line of work although he has with Chava as an assistant *velador* on many construction jobs. It's evident that Pancho wouldn't hurt a flea even though the fleas have not as yet reciprocated. Carole says that Pancho is brown and I say he is cement color. I think Chava is afraid to give him a bath or even get him near water lest his coat harden and he becomes a block of concrete in the shape of a dog.

On another occasion when I was visiting, I noticed a short section of scaffolding at a front corner of the house that looked peculiar. Scaffolding in these parts is often put together from odd planks and boards fastened with nails and bailing wire. What it lacks in sturdiness, I believe, is made up for in the agility of the workers who use it to jump off. There were two large stones on one end of the horizontal plank of the scaffold that the worker stands on. The top of the front wall of the house is about twenty feet above the ground, but at one end it is only about eight feet above the surface. The legs supporting the scaffolding were located at this end and the plank was cantilevered over the twenty-foot drop. I asked Chava what the two big rocks were for, and he scrambled up on the scaffold and demonstrated how he could step out in front of the house twenty or so feet above the ground and put a decorative cornice on the wall. I was flabbergasted at this arrangement that looked more like a diving board than a scaffold. I told him he should be careful. "I am, I am," he replied, "that's why I've got those big stones on one end."

A Little Bit More About the House We're Building

This house is just about the most exciting thing we've undertaken in a long time so, please, bear with us if this is getting to be too much. The instructions we wrote and gave to our architect specified that we wanted a house that was to be very Mexican in appearance. The weather here is pleasant much of the time, and we want to be able sit outside and talk, read, visit, play cards, eat, have a drink and entertain friends. An ample-sized terraza would take advantage of Guanajuato's fine weather and would be a main feature of our new house. We specified an L-shaped, covered porch adjoining the house on two sides, thus permitting a choice of sun or shade throughout the day. We also want to be able to step out of our living room onto the terraza to enjoy the splendid view from the front of the house, or move out of the dining room to eat *al fresco*.

Another feature we wanted was to be able to step out of the master bedroom or the guest bedroom into a garden. The house should be designed with attention to orientation to the sun, winds, and seasons. There were a few things we wanted that are not so common in the houses in Guanajuato, one being copper hot water pipes within plastic PVC pipes to provide insulation. This way hot water can reach the shower without our having to wait for the brick walls to heat up. Guanajuato receives an average of twenty-nine inches of rain per year, but it has a nine-month dry season. Our idea was to capture the rainwater off the roof and store it in a large cistern for watering the garden. Efren designed a cistern large enough to water the front half of our yard for six months. For some reason the idea of the plastic encapsulated copper tubing never got implemented, and the architect couldn't do a lot about the winds, but, all in all, we believe we are getting most of what we wanted and a lot more, solely due to the architect's knowledge and design capabilities. The terraza has eight columns carved for us at the same shop in Patzquaro, Michoacan where we had our carved doors made. These wooden posts support a large heavy beam called "*la madrina*," which actually means godmother, but in this context, I suppose, is the mother beam. This beam holds up the exposed *vigas*, slanted joists that support the clay tile roof. The end of each *viga* is sawed into a decorative end piece. Mexican design, with its Spanish and Moorish antecedence, seems to abhor plainness. One of the interesting things to observe in Guanajuato, as throughout Mexico, is the amazing variety of decoration on buildings. One sees this on some of the humblest of homes as well as the grandest of old haciendas. Quite a switch for Carole and me in what we have known and liked, but I think part of the enchantment of living in Mexico is to go ahead and take pleasure in all of this decoration.

Security is something else we wanted for this house. Carole and I feel personally safe in Guanajuato. The people are helpful, caring and honest with one teeny, weenie exception. If something looks like it is not being cared for; if no one is around and it looks easy to steal, it's likely gone. It would be hard to imagine someone confronting either of us in Guanajuato for the purpose of robbery, but it's not hard to imagine unattended property disappearing. We recognize that there can be no absolute security, but certain measures can be taken to enhance it. First, we believe that the lot is in the safest area in Guanajuato. Because of the topography, it is difficult to enter the subdivision except through one entrance. The surrounding land uses and neighborhood pose no threat. In fact, I dare say, miscreants would classify the area as being in the "not robber friendly" category. The boulevard that leads to our subdivision contains no dwellings or businesses, only the central fire station, the Supreme Judicial Tribunal, and the Office of the Prosecutor General of the State of Guanajuato.

In the front of our property the workers have constructed a stone wall and a gate entrance. The plans call for a wall all the way around our property. Because of its great height and closeness to the front of the lot, the terraza is a perfect spot for hot cauldrons of oil to pour on any invading hordes. We considered using hot salsa instead of boiling oil, but this might attract a crowd with tortillas in hand.

The residents of our subdivision contribute money to pay the city police for a special night patrol of the eight houses and twenty some lots in this development. Prior to this, we had a night watchman, but the residents opted to dismiss him in favor of a contract with Guanajuato PD. I had some concerns as to whether this would be a better arrangement than the watchman had even in spite of his problem of occasionally sleeping on the job. My concern was that the police would drive by a couple of times each night and that would be the extent of their protective services. However, a few weeks ago I drove to our site at night to check to see if the street light in front of our place was working. Out of the dark came a policeman on foot who greeted me politely. He was dressed in a blue black uniform with shiny black boots and a shiny black Uzi gun. Nowhere do I recall in the chapter "Designing The Safe Neighborhood," a primer we used in City Planning 102, any mention of Uzi-armed foot patrols. (Would someone who receives these newsletters please let the Department of Urban and Regional Planning at the University of Wisconsin know about this. Armed watchmen may be an idea that just might work.)

Four Hundred Year Family Reunion

The Montemayors have not been particularly noted for big family reunions, at least on the Wisconsin side. A family reunion of Monts in recent years would probably be limited to immediate family members and the cat. So it was a big surprise to receive a fax one morning from a Colonel E. Montemayor, (USAF Retired) in San Antonio, Texas. The fax invited Carole and me to a reunion of Montemayors to celebrate the 400th anniversary of the founding of the city of Monterrey, Mexico by our ancestor, Don Diego de Montemayor, in 1596.

I was surprised how Colonel Montemayor got my name and fax number here in the mountains of central Mexico. Something impressed me though about the scheduling of this event. Zounds! After four centuries, we were all going to get together?

The event takes place November 8–11. Included during the four days are a reception at the Hotel Monterrey (owned by Luis Montemayor, so we are getting a special rate), a historical presentation on the founding of the City of Monterrey, visits to a museum, a floral presentation at the statue of don Diego, a sealing of a time capsule that will be unearthed in 2096 at the next reunion (I'll try and make it.), a visit to the Cuatemoc Brewery with a reception in the garden, various Mexican dinners with entertainment by folkloric singers and dancers, and a cock fight (simulated). There will be a special mass in the Cathedral for the descendants. The Archbishop of Monterrey, the mayors of the cities of Monterrey, San Antonio, Texas, and several smaller towns have been invited. The priest giving the mass is also a descendant of don Diego. We will meet Governor Montemayor of the neighboring state of Coahuila. We will visit three nearby smaller towns that are hot beds of Montemayors and decedents of *el fundador, Don Diego de Montemayor.* Included in the program are music and dinner at a restored hacienda and a visit to the cemetery where, I believe, my great grandparents are buried. Returning to Monterrey, there will be a concert for us by the City of Monterrey band in a plaza by the old City Hall. The reunion sounds *fabulosa, no?* So, we're going. There's just one thing I wonder about. How do you simulate a cockfight? Do you suppose they use old hens?

8

April, 1997

400th Year Reunion, Beans, Jokes in Spanish, Big Move Into New House, Chava's Story, Neighborhood Meeting, The Garden

400th Year Reunion

There we were, Charlie and Carole Montemayor, surrounded by four hundred Montemayors. We were all there to celebrate the four hundredth anniversary of the founding of the City of Monterrey by our illustrious ancestor, Don Diego de Montemayor. To be precise, not all of the four hundred guests were Montemayors. As explained to us, eleven other families joined Don Diego in the founding of the city and their descendants, too, were invited to this reunion. The first evening's reception found us checking each other's noses to see just who among us had an authentic Montemayor nose. Later, someone in the crowd called out "Señor Montemayor!" whereupon several hundred heads, many with very similar noses, turned simultaneously in response.

We visited the bronze statue of *el fundador*. Standing fourteen feet tall and back-dropped by a one hundred foot wide mosaic mural depicting the founding of Monterrey, Don Diego cut an impressive figure. I have to say I was very proud to be a Montemayor. I especially liked that my ancestor was regarded as a *fundador* rather than a less politically correct *conquistador*. Altogether it was quite magnificent. Even though Don Diego held the rank of captain general, I like to think that the forward-extending sword he held was meant to portray his pointing the way rather than one of leading a charge.

The reunion included presentations by municipal chroniclers. These are persons appointed by the city to keep an official record of local history. What a splendid idea for a city like my hometown of Madison. Madisonians would gain a better understanding of how the city came to be and the forces and events that made it the wonderful place it is today. It might also mean one less PhD. historian driving a cab.

When the Spanish came to the Monterrey area, the territory was inhabited by one or more of the many Chichemeca Indian tribes, none Spanish-friendly. Two previous attempts to establish a hacienda and village on the site of Monterrey ended in ashes. The fact that the leaders of previous efforts were cruel to the indigenous people didn't make it any easier for don Diego. The chroniclers explained that don Diego treated the Indians better but also approached his goal unlike others: he had the right **documents.** This is very important in Mexico, as we have come to understand. He came with a royal charter and a proclamation written with a high sense of mission and confidence. It proclaims in part:

> *In the name of Almighty God, and the Virgin Mary, Mother of God, with this charter of foundation, come I, Diego de Montemayor, treasurer of the royal treasury and Lieutenant Governor of the New Kingdom of Leon...and in the name of your Royal Majesty, Our Lord, and by virtue of the power you possess, I have founded this metropolitan city, Our Lady of Monterrey,...on the twentieth day of September, fifteen hundred and ninety six.*

It probably didn't hurt his chances of success to name the city after the Viceroy, the Count of Monterrey, and, to be on the safe side, he included "Our Lady" the Virgin Mary, in the title of the city, accomplishing all in the name of the King. Was it courage or rashness for Don Diego and eleven families to travel across the Mexican desert in ox drawn wagons and horseback to found the site of Monterrey. Was this feat something grand—or just grandiose? Daniel Burnham in his introduction to the famous 1909 plan for Chicago said: "Make no little plans. They have no magic to stir men's blood...make big plans; aim high in hope and work." I think Don Diego may have said the same thing three hundred years earlier. Today, Monterrey is a burgeoning metropolis of three and one half million people.

The reunion included visits to three smaller nearby towns. The chroniclers explained that while don Diego probably never visited any of these places, that by the third generation, Montemayors had settled there and many still remain to this day. It surprised me to learn that three of my great grandparents, including one from my mother's side, were each born in one of these three places. For about three hundred years, my forbears remained in Zuazua, Marin, and Higueres, three towns only a few miles apart. Although neater and more prosperous than the small towns near Guanajuato, they weren't particularly interesting. What was the economic base of these places? What was it that kept these folks from leaving? At the cemetery I noticed that about a quarter of the graves were Montemayors and virtually every one had a great slab of marble about six inches thick covering each grave site attesting to the occupant's prosperity; or perhaps the relatives wanted to make sure they stayed in place.

The City of Monterrey intends to make Don Diego's founding into an annual international festival. In the meantime, the talk among those attending the reunion was to meet again in Toledo, Spain in 2000.

Beans

One of the things we especially enjoy about living in Mexico is the food. The freshness and wide variety of fruits, vegetables, meats, seafood, cheeses, breads and condiments, and the methods of preparation continue to amaze us. The dishes we have enjoyed most embrace the Spanish and Indian fare, as well as the highly distinctive cuisine of Mexico's separate regions. I'm sure we have barely scratched the surface. As Diana Kennedy in her cookbook, *The Art of Mexican Cooking* points out: "The foods of regional Mexico are in a gastronomic world of their own, a fascinating and many-faceted world, but alas, far too many people outside of Mexico still think of them as an overly large platter of mixed messes, smothered with shrill tomato sauce, sour cream, and grated yellow cheese, preceded by a dish of mouth searing sauce and greasy, deep fried chips. Although these do represent some of the basic foods of Mexico—in name only—they have been brought down to their lowest common denominator north of the border."

I recently conducted a small-scale research project concerning comparative food digestibility; I can share my findings. Before we had digital satellite TV, we watched Mexican television. Like TV in America, there is plenty of advertising on TV here, ranging from quaint products, such as Vicks Vaporub, to those exercise machines that build up your abs. It occurred to me that one rarely, if ever, saw commercials for antacid medications in Mexico. The American TV programs we now receive on our satellite system are fairly inundated with commercials advertising some type of stomach relief product. There must be a lot of burning stomachs and distressed pyloric valves in America. I checked with two drug stores here to see what they had in way of antacids expecting to find a fulsome variety. Both stores offered a single product choice. I consider this research as sort of an acid test, and I rest my case. The food we eat here is delicious and quite digestible.

In future additions of **Letter From Mexico** I intend to include accounts of some of our culinary adventures. But for openers, let me start with the lowly bean. At one end of the *Mercado Embajadoras* (Lady Ambassador's Market) we see a few stands where they sell beans, lentils, rice and similar dry foods. One day Carole and I were examining this amazing array of dry foods displayed in open baskets. Carole was attracted to one tray of small yellow seeds. Neither of us could place this particular item. As accomplished shoppers at this market, and budding connoisseurs of the foods of Mexico, we both picked up a small quantity of these seeds and started to chew on them. The flavor was unrevealed as the seeds were hard as a rock. Carole asked the Indian woman who tended this stand what they were. With only a faint hint of a smile, the old lady said, "That's bird-seed." Well, how were we supposed to know?

In this particular market, as throughout Mexico, there are an astonishing variety of beans from which to choose. To name a few: the black *vercruzano,* the deep yellow *canarios,* the brownish *sabinos,* the white *aluvas,* and our favorite, *flor de mayo*, or mayflower bean. For those who really know their beans, and appreciate subtle differences, there is a *flor de junio*, which is a June flower bean. Cheppa cooks our beans in a clay pot on top of the stove. They are simply delicious and we have them almost every day with *la comida,* the big afternoon meal. I know some of you may be thinking that while you like beans the gas they produce is embarrassing. What I hope you might learn from this little dissertation is that if you eat beans regularly, say every other day, natural enzymes build up in your stomach achieving a certain equilibrium thus eliminating the offensive gaseous condition. This certainly has proved to be the case for me and for millions of people who eat beans in this country. Absent this enzymatic process you can be sure that there would be another hole in the ozone layer hovering above Mexico blasted out by billowing effusions of methane gas.

A few weeks ago for some unknown reason, our household went an entire week without any beans. One night, I became frightened and worried when I heard a giant sucking noise fearing that a certain reverse process was now taking place. As it turned out my fears were unfounded. The noise came from Ross Perot upon his discovering that the poor, penniless Mexicans were buying expensive Mercedes Benz trucks and busses as fast as Germany could export them.

Jokes in Spanish

I probably shouldn't, but occasionally I like to try to tell a joke in Spanish. It must be painful to the listener as he or she tries to help me out by guessing at the missing or wrong words. But the other day, I got off what I guess was a pretty good one. I was visiting with the construction workers at our house near the end of their lunch break. They were sitting around a fire roasting boiled pea-nuts—very tasty, by the way. The *maestro* mentioned to the four or five workers that I was a good jalapeno eater and told them that when we had had our little "feed" for the workers I had popped a whole chili pepper in my mouth. Of course, I had broken the pepper open and removed all the seeds so it wasn't really that much of a challenge. However, with the camaraderie that seems to bring people together when they sit around an open fire, I felt I was among friends and could tell my little story. I related that in the United States, in the state of New Mexico, (one of the more knowledgeable workers interrupted to explain to the others that this was someplace in Texas), an American scientist had perfected a jalapeno pepper that wasn't hot, or in Spanish, *que no pica*. Of course, this is per-fectly logical to us Americans, but the workers started to howl at this concept, looking at each other, slapping their knees and repeating *jalapeños que no pica*.

Recently, during a visit from my cousin Emma Vidal, her husband Henry, and daughter, Pat Roberts, we all went to San Miguel for some shopping. Carole and I were looking for door handles and other hardware for our house and became separated from our cousins. The day was warm and we stopped to quench our thirst with a soft drink at a bar. Tending the bar was a cute young *señorita*. In an effort to exchange some pleasantries, I asked her if they had live music, and she explained the week's schedule that seemed to consist of a different type of Mexican music each evening of the week. She looked quite young for this job and yet she seemed proficient in her work. I was curious about her age but felt I shouldn't ask for fear she might be underage and would be embarrassed. What I asked her in Spanish, or thought I asked her, was how long she had been working at this place. What I probably said was more like how long are you working here. She said she gets off at 6:30. Carole, of course, was laughing at my predicament. "Ooh, nooh, nooh", I said. "Let me try this again. How many **years** have you worked here?"

Big Move Into New House

We were pretty excited when Efrén Fonseca, our architect, told us to get ready to move; our house was now nearing completion. We were all packed by December 15 and set for the move to our new Mexican house. The construction crew would do the actual move. Only a few things were still lacking—the three skylights, cab-inets, outside paint, half the inside and outside wall lamps, some roof tile, part of the driveway and a few other things. The lease on our house we were renting ended December 31, which coincidentally, turned out to be moving day. Here we come, ready or not. Months ago, we had invited Gus and Marina Garcia of Austin Texas to stay with us on their next visit to GTO. Coincidentally, their trip was scheduled for the end of December, a date we thought would find us fairly well settled in the new place. Gus is a member of the City Council and Deputy Mayor of Austin Texas. The Garcias are a delightful and an unflappable couple who took all of our house moving problems in stride. Derek and Elisa Young invited them over to their place for the latter part of their visit so it all worked out.

One of the interesting features of our new place is the driveway. As I have previously mentioned, our lot is quite steep and in order to maximize the view and minimize (ha ha) the number of steps, the house is set back from the street and is reached by a driveway that starts out almost parallel with the street and then makes a sharp, graduating "U" turn all the while gaining altitude. Even with this winding ascension, the grade of the driveway is about 22 percent. Our friends, Derek and Elisa Young, are building a house next to us, using the same architect and much of the same work force. Construction of the last meter at the end of the "U" turn of our drive had to be delayed so that the wall supporting the driveway could be integrated with the Young's home. The workers placed a few rocks on the curve to discourage me driving too close to the edge where it drops off about fourteen feet. The stones, of course, denied me the last eight inches making it all the more necessary to get up some speed to make that grade. Now there are plenty of steep drives and streets in GTO, and I don't think that we have the steepest, but I believe we might be the only people in the world who have a driveway with a banked curve. Do you remember those carnival shows where a daredevil would ride a motorcycle in a velodrome? (It's odd that I remember the word "velodrome" when I have trouble remembering where I left my car keys.) Well, a velodrome is an indoor arena with a circular track that is steeply banked. The motorcycle travels horizontally and parallel with the earth's surface. I'm not saying that our driveway is the same as a section of velodrome, but going up the grade makes one feel ALIVE AND YOUNG AGAIN. To reach the top requires the "big momentum," as they say in politics. I told Carole that now that they have completed that last meter of driveway, something is missing from our lives. She said, "Yes—FEAR."

We love the house but I'm sure it would not appeal to everyone. Efrén has proudly told us that there isn't another house like ours in all of Guanajuato. I'm not sure what that means, but I think it's good. Recently an engineer/developer from nearby Irapuato visited our place and wants Efrén to build a house like ours in his fancy development in his generally flat city. After he figures in the cost of building a steep hill like ours he may want to change his mind. Not everything turned out as we wanted. One of the prime examples of something that went awry is the woodwork.

Long before we had decided on building a house, we thought it would be a good idea to have a local woodworker build us a large cabinet to hold the TV, stereo components, CDs, tapes, and Carole's needlework. It was a big job (2′ x 5′ x 6′, total cost $200) and required $100 of wood, which I paid in advance to some *carpinteros*. That's what they call woodworkers here. There were other small jobs that we needed such as a bench and some furniture repairs. The *carpinteros* I had hired did a beautiful job on our small projects; however, as time went by, I hadn't heard of any progress on the large cabinet. I looked up the receipt the *carpintero* had given me on my deposit and was dismayed to see no address or phone number. Moreover, the serial number on the receipt was Number 1, leading me to believe that they acquired the receipt book just for us, or, they didn't have much business. As our house plans evolved we decided on a built-in niche for the TV and stereo, so we wouldn't need the cabinet anymore. My $100 investment had probably been spent for food rather than wood, so I didn't really expect a refund, but I suggested to Efrén that we have the *carpinteros* work off the $100 by doing some other construction on the house. Efrén said he would find the *carpinteros* for me.

Efrén went ahead and hired them to do all the woodwork on the house. That's not exactly what I had in mind. When I first observed the *carpinteros* at work I was pleased at what I saw. They were able to take louvered closet doors which Efrén and I had purchased and rebuild them into a variety of smaller cabinet doors. It was wonderful to see them hand planeing and sawing the wood. And those of you who know the wonderful smell of freshly sawn pine will appreciate the satisfaction I felt from this combination of good wood and honest hand labor. It wasn't until later that Carole and I began to notice some of their deficiencies and finally their truly outrageous craftsmanship.

Our house, like most all the houses here, is of masonry construction. To attach doorframes or anything of wood you need to drill a hole in the cement wall and stick a plug or anchor into the hole so that the screw can be firmly attached. To my dismay, the *carpinteros* broke off a strip of wood and pounded it into the hole in our beautiful house. It all looked so slipshod. I went to a hardware store to buy them some plastic plugs and as I was completing the transaction I told the clerk about the crummy *carpinteros* and how they would jam a splinter of wood into the hole. The clerk politely told me, "But *Señor*, that really makes a very strong fastener, and that is the way they do it here. Of course, if you want to buy the plastic or lead anchors we have them here and I would be glad to sell them to you." That made me reflect on my criticism of their work methods. Perhaps I should let them do their work in their own way.

Although I know that the *carpinteros* probably never had the advantage of watching Bob Villa on American TV, I was dismayed to see these guys pounding perfectly good screws (I had paid good money for) into the cement walls-rather than screwing them in as Bob Villa would do. Some of these were beautiful brass screws, pounded askew, some protruding out of hinges or door locks. Hinges are often set double depth so that only one side of the hinge would have to be set in. The men worked very slowly measuring everything several times but seldom getting anything square. My disrespect turned into a suppressed rage.

Chava's Story

Remember Chava? He's the *velador,* the night watchman who guards the construction project from the time the workers leave until their return. Chava also works a regular forty-four hour per week shift on the Young's construction crew. From our terraza I can watch the work on the Young's house. It was pretty obvious that all of the workmen worked hard, but Chava was outstanding, working harder than all the others. He did a wide variety of tasks and he did them well. Cement work, brick laying, tile work, painting, shoveling and digging. When doing pick ax work, he would remove his shirt and one could see the full force of his glistening lean body and powerful muscles as he took full swings at removing the crumbling rock that makes up the soil here. At night, with machete in hand, he would always be ready at the gate to open it for us when we drove up. It was as if he never slept. One morning I was surprised by his visit to our door. His head hung down as he explained to me that he was being dismissed from his construction job at our neighbor's. He said he didn't have any other job prospects and wondered if we could use someone to help with things in the house. I asked why he had been dismissed and he said that they were cutting back and that while he could stay as *velador* he didn't have a job during the day. I said I would check with Efrén and that we might be able to use someone to finish some things and make certain changes. Efrén later explained that Chava had been fired by the *maestro* for fighting with the other workers. He told us that Chava would go on and on about how he was always on time, he worked harder than anyone else, that he didn't drink and he didn't smoke—unlike the others. Chava talks a lot and repeats himself four or five times. I think this can probably get on someone's nerves particularly when he is claiming how good he is and accusing others of misdeeds. Efrén said that no one had a complaint about his work; only it was impossible to have him around because he caused so much trouble with his talking.

Carole diagnosed Chava as being a hyperactive workaholic. We have always tried to be socially responsible and so we decided to hire Chava in spite of his "handicap." He asked for, and we gave him, a ten percent wage increase and a day off to visit his family in the country. He then went to work. Both Carole and I were delighted to have this human dynamo helping us. He was productive and careful with his work and he was meticulous about cleaning up his work site. Chava was an excellent worker in every way. The sad thing is that, one day, when we returned from a trip to Leon, Chava had packed up and left. No explanation. It seemed to me that all those extra hours of work Chava so desperately wanted finally caught up with him.

As a replacement, Efrén recommended another worker to be assigned directly to us, a young fellow named Juan. Carole says he's cute. It turns out that Juan's father is one of the *maestros*. His uncle *Juan* is another *maestro*, and his grandfather, *Don Juan*, is a mason on the project. *Don Juan* is sixty-six years old and although he has a young assistant, Tito, *Don Juan* carries the big stones just like his young helper. *Don Juan* has a soft-spoken manner that effuses a sense of kindness, patience and sincerity. One feels humbled in his presence.

Neighborhood Meeting

Loma de Pozuelos is the name of the street and subdivision where we live. There are eight occupied houses on our street that form a loop about six tenths of a mile long. Someone from Guadalajara is building a fancy place around the bend from us occupying four lots. It is only two bedrooms but will have a home theater and a swimming pool. Recently, we were invited to a meeting of the neighbors to discuss some changes with the sub-divider. He has been paying to have the street cleaned and now he wants us to assume this cost. The custom, or law, in Guanajuato, perhaps all of Mexico, is that every owner must keep the street in front of his place clean. Street sweeping in residential areas is not a municipal service. One sees maids and housewives out front of their house every morning throwing some water on the street and then sweeping it down. Also discussed was trash removal. Some of our neighbors disapprove of persons who put out their trash too early as its unsightly appearance also attracts animals. The city trash truck comes by six days a week. Someone on the truck rings a hand bell; you have about five minutes to get your trash out before they return. I don't always hear the bell so I have to guess when the truck arrives. For me, it's all a matter of timing. The other issue was to change the night surveillance from city police to a private service.

The neighbors all seemed quite nice and friendly. I was a bit confused by the status of our street, which has two posts and a chain across it at the entrance to our subdivision. I asked whether it was a private or a public road. Loma de Pozuelos, I was told, is actually a public street, but the neighborhood is treating it as if it were a private street in order to retain more control. These are tricky concepts for Americans living here.

I mention these items to give you some idea of what it is like here at Loma de Pozuelos. An urbanologist I once knew maintained that a good way to judge the quality of life of a city, and presumably a neighborhood, is to monitor the kind of problems discussed in letters to the editor, public meetings, etc. I would have to say that life is not bad here except for the difficulty in hearing the trash truck when it makes its rounds.

Besides Elisa and Derek Young who live next door to us, the neighbors we know best are Pedro and Mattie Buchanan. Pedro is retired from the Mexican telephone company where he served as a public relations official. Both Pedro and Mattie speak English and have been very nice to us. Their home is a fairly new Victorian-style house. However, with TelMex's reputation you can be sure Pedro had his work cut out for him. Recently I failed to pay our phone bill because no bill was sent to us. Consequently, our service was cut off. To restore it, I had to go to the phone company and wait in line outdoors for half an hour to pay my bill. Now it's very pleasant outdoors, but to wait in a line a block long so that I can pay a bill [never received] with only one open teller window seems not the best way to prepare for telephone competition from AT&T and MCI scheduled to arrive here in May. While there was only one teller collecting money, another employee was assigned to direct traffic in the overflowing parking lot.

In back of us live *Señor Villaseñor* and his wife. He is an attorney whose hobby is collecting restored classic autos. While he works in a rather dingy office in the center of the city, the Villaseñors live in a modern, almost starkly modern, house that we visited at one of the neighborhood meetings. The inside of their house looked like it might have popped out of a book on modern Mexican architecture. The use of glass and space was lavish, the quality of materials and craftsmanship were superb, and the colors used were daring and stunning, Mrs. Villaseñor is attractive, young looking and seemed a part of the home design. Later we learned that the joy of her life were visits from her grandchildren. We never would have guessed that she was a grandma six times over. Stepping out of this elegant, modern and austere home onto a walled back yard we encountered a plain grassy area with a couple of swing sets. I bet the architect didn't approve. Other neighbors include Mr. and Mrs. Bilbao. They own a string of small hardware stores in GTO and the two of them live in what looks like a French provincial style house with two wings in the form of a "Y". I wonder if they each have a separate wing.

A few lots away is an American family, Penny and Jim Wright and their two boys. Jim is a retired U.S. Air Force officer whose assignments have taken them to various parts of the world. Penny told us that when they lived in Spain they bought an old windmill and remodeled it into a house. She didn't mention why, but they still own it. Jim is managing a company that he and some friends organized. They buy hides from Chile and prepare them here for the furniture trade in North Carolina. They will be moving into a house they bought in Marfil. Some time ago we were asked by a realtor to look at a house that had a shooting range in the lower level. Well, the Wrights bought this place. They are going to add a swimming pool, and in a sort of canons to plowshares effort, are making the rifle range into a gymnasium for the boys.

Our house is very modest in comparison to some of those of our neighbors but we think it's more authentic and quite appropriate for Loma de Pozuelos.

The Garden

Neither Carole nor I have ever excelled at gardening. What a shame, because we now live in a place where plants, shrubs and trees grow so profusely that weeds seem to be the ones that get crowded out. One can drive through a poor village and see red and magenta bougainvillea covering walls; flowering shrubs of every color; huge lavender jacaranda trees; and potted plants growing in great profusion adorning the most humble houses. It all appears to be effortless horticulture. To change our status as gardening-challenged, plant-illiterate *gringos*, I bought Carole a book on gardening in Mexico. We may commit inplantacide before we are done, but by gosh, we are going to have some color in our garden if I have to paint the rocks myself. I don't know why, but three *jardineros* who we asked to lay out our garden never returned. Efrén finally convinced us that we could design the garden ourselves. Plants, shrubs and trees started to arrive, mostly ahead of our having the beds ready, but slowly we have started to plant. It's beginning to look rather nice.

9

November 1997

Museums of Guanajuato, Heart Disease, Understanding Mexico, Funerals, The Mexican Elections, Ex-Pat Delegation Issues Admonition, Average Cumulative Income of Americans Living in San Miguel Plunges—Charities Expected to Suffer, Substantial Increase in Average Income of Americans in San Miguel is rumored—Charities May Benefit

Museums of Guanajuato

In a city with only 80,000 people, it is a bit surprising to find nine public museums. And this doesn't count the town, which is something of a museum itself. There's a lot of history here. In the mid-fifteen hundreds, the road from Mexico City to the newly discovered mines in Zacatecas passed near what is now Guanajuato. Some accounts say that a party stopped to rest and eat on top of one of the *cerros* (large hills) near here. They protected their campfire from the winds with some rocks. Much to their surprise the rocks started to melt releasing free silver. This must have been one of the best meals they ever had. A few years later (1554), Guanajuato was founded and named Royal Mines of Guanajuato. In 1619, The King of Spain recognized our town with the title The Very Noble and Very Loyal Villa of Santa Fe, Royal Mines of Guanajuato. But on September 16, 1810, loyalty to Spain, if not the Crown, had pretty much run out and the Mexican War of Independence started. Thirty-four miles east of here in the town of Dolores, Father Hidalgo gave his famous cry for independence (El Grito) and, starting with 300 townsfolk, marched to various nearby towns picking up support along the way. The army of insurgents, now 50,000 strong, (royalists would say rabble,) arrived in Guanajuato on September 28 and took the ***Alhóndiga de Granaditas*** where the Spanish loyalists were holed up. The Alhóndiga is a massive stone building completed by the Spanish in 1798 after twelve years of construction. At that time, it was a granary. To my eye, it looks like it was designed as a fortress. Why, for example, does a granary need a row of small narrow windows high up along the building's perimeter? The Mexican insurgents were unable to penetrate the Alhóndiga until a young Indian, a miner nicknamed *El Pipila*, (Little Turkey), with a slab of stone as a shield and a torch in his right hand, ran up to the great wooden doors and set them afire. The rest is history, and today the ***Alhóndiga de Granaditas*** is a regional history museum that highlights one of Mexico's most heroic battle sites.

Muralist Diego Rivera, who these days is better known as the husband of Frida Khalo, was born in Guanajuato. His family home has been made into the **Diego Rivera Museum**. Another museum is the **Ex Hacienda de San Gabriel de Barrera,** which is a restored hacienda built in the sixteen hundreds of rather baronial style and dimensions. One of the most prominent and centrally located museums is the ***Museo Iconográfico del Quijote*** displaying paintings and sculptures donated by international artists and all having to do with Don Quixote. There is also a natural history museum and by all accounts an outstanding mineralogy and mining museum that I want to visit soon. .

According to an American writer for the English language San Miguel newspaper, the Mummy Museum of Guanajuato (***Museo de las Momias***) is Guanajuato's community embarrassment, not unlike San Miguel's annual running of the bulls patterned after the event in Pamplona Spain. The writer describes this San Miguel event as a bunch of drunks running in front of a herd of bulls in which some runners and spectators get hurt. This event brings a lot of money into San Miguel, and, I suppose, your opinion as to whether this is good or bad depends on whose ox is being gored. Anyway, as for the ***Museo de las Momias,*** all I can say is that tackiness is in the eye of the beholder. Some people love it, some hate it. Carole hates it. I, of course, remain steadfastly nonjudgmental. The Museum adjoins the city cemetery and is enormously popular with visitors to Guanajuato. The proceeds from the museum are substantial all of it going to support housing and social programs for the poor. Apparently, the particular mineral composition of the soil and the arid climate of Guanajuato have had the effect of mummifying bodies buried here. This was discovered in 1865 when some graves were being exhumed. All the bodies are tastefully displayed in glass cases—well, as tastefully as is possible given that there really are no standards for museums of this type. The first time I visited *las Momias*, I left the premises a little faint due to the high altitude of Guanajuato, I'm sure. Several of the mummies on display look like they died screaming; speculation among visitors is that they were buried alive. But as I have later learned, the facial contortions are a result of the desiccation process. Much can be learned from a visit to this museum; for example, mummified male genitalia virtually disappear. So much for paradise. Some visitors from America find *El Museo de las Momias*, I guess, distasteful, even without visiting it. Yet, when *The National Geographic Magazine* published a series of pictures of "The Snow Princess", a young women that was sacrificed and frozen to death in the Andes, they wrote affectionately of her loveliness and of what a wonderful discovery this all was. And some years earlier, when the Egyptian government sent King Tutankhamen on a tour of major US museums, people flocked to admire this old mummy. But poor Guanajuato, when they display not one, but 119 bodies all naturally mummified—no chemicals, no artificial preservatives, no human sacrifices—some people think this is tacky.

My favorite museum is the **Olga Costa-José Chávez Morado Art Museum.** The museum is located away from the center of town in an *ex hacienda* that Olga and José refurbished into their home. The structure has two separate sections about forty feet apart but visually connected by a flying arch from an ancient aqueduct. After Olga's death, one section of the house was donated to the city for a museum containing their paintings and a collection of pre-Hispanic colonial artifacts. José, who is the more famous of the two artists, still lives in the remaining section. He was recently honored in Mexico City, and, as I understand it, was presented with a commemorative postage stamp. I can only hope that one of his paintings, or José's likeness, appeared on the stamp less this tribute turn out to be embarrassingly small for someone so accomplished. The city department of cultural affairs sponsors monthly concerts in the museum. We attended one of these concerts. A classical guitarist played Bach, Villa-Lobos and some flamenco music. It was lovely. After the free concert, wine was served in a handsome courtyard garden to the guests of the city of Guanajuato. The design of the garden and the selection of plant material gave us ideas for our own garden. In the middle of the courtyard is a large clay pot with an enormous jade plant called *siempre vive* (always lives). Olga's ashes are interned in this urn simply marked with her name and years of life.

Artists, I suppose, like the rest of us, can be generous or stingy. José Chávez Morado, born in Silao a few miles south of Guanajuato, has just donated money to Silao so that they may purchase the house where he was born. This home will be used as a museum to display his donated collection of paintings. This generosity made me recall an incident involving Georgia O'Keeffe. Ms. O'Keeffe was born in Sun Prairie, Wisconsin, a few miles north of Madison. Except for Wilber Renk, a successful producer of hybrid seed corn, and Jimmy, a copycat groundhog that makes long-range weather forecasts (a la Puxtahtawnee Phil), Sun Prairie is not known for having produced many luminaries. In an effort to enhance the city's image, the Sun Prairie Chamber of Commerce organized an event inviting Miss O'Keeffe to cut the ribbon on a street renamed in her honor. Her response: send me $5,000 and I'll show up.

Heart Disease

For some time I have been reading articles about the tantalizing information concerning the low incidence of coronary disease among Frenchman and their high consumption of wine. In an article in the February 5, 1996, issue of Newsweek, I read about Morly Safer's 1991 visit to Lyons France and his "60 Minutes" story on "The French Paradox." Despite their high-fat diet, Safer reported the French have only one-third our rate of heart attacks. To explain the Paradox, he held up a glass of red wine. Safer should have held up a glass of saki or tequila instead of the wine. The Newsweek article contained a table (copied below) "edited" by me so that I can show that instead of listing the countries in order of their wine consumption, I have put them in order of their incidence of heart disease—low incidence of death on top and high incidence on the bottom. As can be seen on the table, Japan, with 34.7 deaths per 100,000 and Mexico, with 36.4 deaths are both very low in the incidence of coronaries. France is 68% higher than Mexico, and the U.S. is a whopping five times higher than Mexico. Wouldn't you know it, CBS ran all the way to France to put this story together, and Mexico is just an easy wade across the river.

	Wine Liters Per Capita	Beer Liters Per capita	Liquor Liters Per capita	Life ex- pectancy	Heart Disease *
Japan	1.0	55.0	2.1	79	34.7
Mexico	0.2	50.4	0.8	73	36.4
France	63.5	40.1	2.5	78	61.1
Italy	58.0	25.1	0.9	78	61.1
Switzerland	46.0	65.0	1.7	78	106.4
Australia	15.7	102.1	1.2	78	173.0
U.S.A.	8.9	87.8	2.0	76	176.0
Britain	12.2	100.0	1.5	77	199.7
Czech Republic	1.7	140.1	1.0	73	283.1

Russia	2.7	17.1	3.8	69	373.6

* Deaths per 100,000
Source: World Health Organization

Understanding Mexico

Scotty Reston, long time Washington bureau chief for the New York Times, once wrote that Americans would do anything for Mexico—except <u>read about it</u>. As I see it, Americans don't need to read and learn about Mexico because we come here with such an insightful understanding of this country. In fact, we understand it better than the Mexicans do; they are too close to the country and its problems to really understand it. Ask a Mexican some question about his country and he will try to explain how complicated that question is, or how sometimes it's this way and sometimes it's that way. Americans on the other hand are not so confused. We have a better perspective of the situation because we live close to Mexico, but not actually in it—analogous to how we know what's wrong with our neighbors' kids while remaining baffled about our own.

It all boils down to two fundamental concepts that we use to explain just about anything one might encounter in Mexico.

CONCEPT #1: Mexico is a poor country.
CONCEPT #2: Mexican males are macho.

That's it folks. These two concepts explain everything one could ever ask about Mexico. Now the Mexicans are under the illusion that their country is rich—rich but exploited by some special group, usually foreign. I think I know why Mexicans fail to realize that their country is poor. The reason for this misconception has to do with an historical event that took place right here in Guanajuato. In the center of town, on the *Plaza de la Paz*, there is a large government building with a plaque indicating that this is the 16th Circuit Federal Judicial Tribunal, in other words, the Federal courthouse. There is a second plaque indicating that during August and September 1803, at this site, Baron Alexander Von Humbolt stayed in the house of the Count of Valenciana. Geographers regard Von Humbolt as the founder of modern geography, a systematic study. The Baron did an extensive five-year study of Spanish America with Guanajuato being one of the last places he visited. Mexico, he said, was rich, and he gave the Mexicans the recipe for success: fewer taxes, more trade, and better government.

Not in their sweetest dreams would American congressman working on reforming the IRS or fat cat taxpayers in the United States ever hope to have what Mexico has managed with its user-friendly tax system. According to an article in the Wall Street Journal, only one person, during the several decades that Mexico has had an Income Tax, has ever gone to jail for an income tax violation. And not only that, but the national sales tax, called IVA, to the best of my knowledge, is voluntary. I'm not kidding. As long as the seller and buyer agree, you don't have to pay the 15% IVA. Only retired bureaucrats like me worry about how they raise enough money to provide for "better government."

Well, back to Humboldt. Instead of staying in the mansion of a Count in one of the richest cities in the world at that time, he should have spent time in the U.S. If he had, his report would have concluded that Mexico was poor, poor, poor. He was really out of his element. Humboldt should have stayed with what was current. There is a covered archway in the Baron's honor named *Arcos de Alejandro Humbolt* extending about 200 feet connecting two of the principal streets in the city. At one end is the *Plaza de la Paz* where you will find the site of the mansion where he stayed. At the other end of the archway, you will find the site of the Royal Prison, where he should have been held for so completely misleading this country. (The building now houses an office that distributes state planning agency reports.)

Let me give you some examples of how these two concepts, poor country and macho males, can be used to answer virtually any question about Mexico:

Q1. Why is that young father, like so many others I see, caring a baby in his arms?

Ans.: You have to understand that Mexican males are basically macho and only a <u>very</u>, <u>very</u> macho male would let himself be seen carrying a baby.

Q2. Why is that baby over there so happy and contented?

Ans.: Mexican families are so poor they can't afford things with which to spoil their children. When parents are poor like that, all they can do is play with their children. Naturally, the kids love it and are happy, but it's really a sad thing that they are so poor and don't have the money to enjoy life like our kids do.

Q3. Why is that child over there throwing a tantrum?

Ans.: That little boy was taught at a very early age to be macho and that includes throwing fits. **But that child is not a boy; it's a little girl!** Well in that case, remember that Mexico is a very poor country and the parents have nothing to feed their children. The kid is probably starving. That's why she is crying.

Q4. Why does Mexico have so many billionaires?

Ans.: Well, Mexico is a very poor country and they can't afford a middle class so they have to put most of their money in nine or ten billionaires.

Q5. Why do Mexican women go with their husbands and boyfriends to bull fights?

Ans.: As you know, bullfighting is very much a macho thing and this machismo rubs off from males onto females. Besides, many of the women who go to these *corridas* are named Veronica and attend only to learn how to avoid the dreaded *picador*.

Q6. Why did Mexico lose the war with the Americans resulting in the loss of half of its territory?

Ans.: Mexicans have always been very macho and they thought it would be sissy to fight Americans with canons or any weapons that were less than a hundred years old so they got whomped. And as for the loss of California, a lot of them think they came out ahead. After all, Mexico never ended up with all those salad bars or a guy named Ricardo Nixon as *el Presidente*.

Q7. Why does Mexico have so many ancient pyramids and historic buildings?

Ans.: Mexico, as a very poor country, has not been able to raise enough cash to sufficiently develop and pave over all of its deterioration. When a country has practically nothing it really doesn't have much choice but to retain its old pyramids even if they are terribly antiquated and inefficient.

Q8. Why are days in Mexico so sunny?

Ans.: Mexico, as I have said, is a very poor country and if it were not for the warmth of the sun there wouldn't be a Mexico. The people wouldn't be able to afford anything to keep them warm so instead of being Mexicans they would be Panamanians where it is always warm.

Q9. Why are nights in Mexico so chilly?
Ans.: Mexicans are very macho and living in a place where it gets cold at night lets them display their machismo.

Q10. Why do the Mexican's eat hot spicy food?
Ans.: Mexico is a very poor country and all your really good food goes to Hormel, Dinty Moore's and Cambell's, big companies that can afford the best stuff. Mexicans have to survive on what's left over and that consists of food too hot to eat. But they don't complain a lot, because they're very, very macho.

The Mexican Elections

Everyone here seemed pleased with the national elections. For the first time in more than seventy years the opposition political parties out-polled the ruling PRI party in the last congressional elections. Now Mexico is able to enjoy divided government, which, of course, in the United States is referred to as gridlock. In addition, most observers were pleased at how clean the elections were in comparison to times past. This is not to say that there was no political hanky panky. I personally know of three instances where the heavy hand of the ruling party took unfair advantage of its power and position in an attempt to affect the outcome of the election. The first example involved the President himself and resulted in loud protests from leaders of the opposition parties. President Zedillo was accused of taking unfair advantage of his position by <u>endorsing members of his own party</u> running for the Chamber of Deputies. Of course I was shocked, shocked, shocked that the President would do such a despicable thing.

The second item I noticed was that the government took unfair advantage of television. The government advertises its programs on television throughout the year. Many of the TV announcements are excellent. The commercials advocating responsible family planning are very well done, as are commercials from the tourism department. I especially like one which shows beautiful shots of migratory birds flying to Mexico, and beautiful scenes of Monarch butterflies arriving in Michoacan, and whales off the Pacific shores with a voice over that went something like this: "Mexico has always welcomed its visitors. For years visitors have come to our country from the north. Mexico is good to tourists and tourists are good for Mexico. Welcome our visitors." At any rate, government departments use TV a lot, so it is not unusual to see announcements on the social security system and other government programs. Just before the election there may have been more of these commercials than usual, but the big complaint of opposition parties was that the commercials were preceded or ended with pictures of the Mexican flag fluttering in the breeze. Now it seems that in Mexico, each political party can choose its own colors and logo but it cannot appropriate [for its use] the same colors used by another party. The PRI, which has been in control for such a long time chose red white and green, the colors of the Mexican flag. Waving that flag with the colors of the PRI party on government commercials was thought to be an unfair campaign tactic.

Another example of corruption I noticed was the arrival in Guanajuato of a platoon of Mexican army soldiers, perhaps twenty soldiers in all. Guanajuato doesn't have a local garrison so the arrival of this group in their impressive Mercedes Benz military truck, just before the elections, was quite noticeable. Although I do not condone corruption of any kind, I have to admit that I was pleased to see the Pride of Mexico planting trees in one of our parks.

Funerals

There are three funeral establishments in town that I know of. One of them seems to be located in an ancient garage-type building that I don't find of much interest. A second one is run by the Department for the Integrated Family, DIF, a marvelous agency organized on the basis of its clientele rather than on the basis of the professions of the agency's staff. Its activities are directed at serving all of the needs of the family: health, education, and welfare. It is also engaged in some entrepreneurial activities that raise money to support its programs. DIF owns most of the parking garages in town and some of the museums. One of the human services it provides is funerals. But the place that catches my eye the most is a *funeria* located on *Avenida Juarez*, the main street. The establishment is probably no more than ten feet by twelve feet in total area. There may be another room in the back. The door is always open and, perhaps, because of my interest in woodworking, I always have to peek in to see how the work is going. Besides that, I tend to get a giggle out of the idea of a funeral parlor operating on an open-door policy. The proprietor is often working on a casket, more often a simple pine box, with great care and attention given to the stapling of cloth inside and out with a profusion of pleats and ruffles. Because of the limited space, the coffins are stacked along the walls, floor to ceiling. In addition to metal and wooden models, the inventory also includes some simple Styrofoam boxes.

People have told me that the Mexican Indian has a different attitude toward death than we do—that they do not fear death—that, in fact, they look forward to and welcome it. I recall hearing the same thing about Asian soldiers in World

War II and the Vietnam War. Well, I for one don't believe it. Dying, it seems to me, has to be, at least, a little bit worse than having a root canal, and it's hard for me to believe that there are many people who look forward to something like that. Assertions that healthy people like to die would be more believable to me if I heard it from the one who is dying, instead of a spokesperson.

I have encountered many funeral processions on the streets of Guanajuato. Given the layout of the town, they are unavoidable. The only realistic route from the churches to the cemetery is along *Avenida Jaurez* that, for over half its length, is a single, one-way traffic lane. The casket rides in the back of a station wagon hearse with the mourners following on foot, most of whom are carrying flowers. Often some form of music accompanies, a drum and bugle corps or mariachis. The drum and bugle corps are interesting, but for some reason, the heavy beat of the drums along with the somewhat discordant bugles leave me with the impression they are marching straight to hell. The mariachis, on the other hand, can bring a tear to my eye as they sing and play *La Golandrina,* the beautiful Mexican song of farewell. It's really very moving to see a procession of one or two hundred people walking with their departed relative or friend for the last time. Shortly after the group crosses the Tepetapa Bridge, a journey of about a mile, the procession stops and the casket is removed from the vehicle. It is now carried by the pallbearers up Tepetapa Street for the last half-mile to the cemetery overlooking the city. Tepetapa Street has a 12% grade and is paved with cobblestone. I am moved and impressed by the commitment of the people who participate. We're not talking about calling up your local **FTD** florist and having them send some flowers. Making this long walk represents a significant personal involvement and commitment. When I see this, I marvel at how anyone could have so many loyal friends who would make the effort. So naturally the question arises, ahem, ahem: when it's my turn, how many folks can I count on to make that climb. Living here in Guanajuato, we have a number of dear friends although most of them are about our age and probably not in good enough shape to do any heavy lifting or walking a mile or so in a funeral procession. To have a successful funeral you need a certain critical mass, i.e., the key is to have enough people. Even in the States, where you're not expected to personally shoulder a casket very far, you still need to have enough people at your funeral to avoid embarrassment. What if the only person who shows up at your funeral is your therapist? Now that's sad. I keep wondering what people here would think of Americans, with our "can do" reputation, if we weren't able to make the grade?

I'm hoping that some of you reading this and who have frequent flyer miles will not squander all of your miles on trips to Disneyland. I'm sure Mickey

Mouse would want you to come to Guanajuato to help me out on this; Mickey will still be there when you get back. Also, you can take in the *Museo de las Momias.* My problem here is that given the 12% grade on Tepetapa, I'm going to need about six or eight people, not including supernumeraries, who are not only in good physical condition but who come in a gradation of heights. Naturally, there would be a certain amount of jostling as we make our way up that cobblestone street; I would hate to start slipping down to one end of the box, so keeping it level is critical. If it would help, I could opt for the Styrofoam jobbie to reduce the load as well as the cost. The more I think about this the more I think immortality is really not a bad idea either. Does anyone have any info on this option?

Ex-Pat Delegation Issues Admonition

Recently, I was visited by a delegation of Americans living in Guanajuato who said they had a matter of concern to discuss with me. The gist of their message was that they had heard that I was writing some type of newsletter. I allowed that I was and would be glad to put them on my mailing list if, perhaps, they would like to contribute toward the postage and printing. They explained this was not exactly what they had in mind. They understood that I was mailing this newsletter back to Wisconsin and that I was describing what a wonderful and interesting place this is. I was telling people about the splendid climate, the paucity of mosquitoes and flies, the interesting architecture, the uniqueness of the city design and road system, the delicious foods, the friendly people, the pretty girls, and on and on. "Well yes," I admitted, "I had described life here as I saw it because I thought there might be people interested in reading this material."

"Listen, Charlie", the delegation leader said to me. "We're concerned. We don't have anything against you or Carole. We're glad that you are part of this community, and we want you to know that it's nothing personal." I knew right then that something was about to hit me. "What we are concerned about is that with your newsletter going out to all those folks in Wisconsin and with all the great things we've heard that you have been saying about this place, pretty soon a bunch of cheeseheads are going to start moving into our town. First one, then another, and pretty soon we are inundated with Wisconsin people. We all agree this town is nice but we want to keep it that way."

I had to smile as I told them not to worry. "I have already thought about this possibility and I have taken very special care to conceal the true identity and location of where we live. I would never be careless about this." I explained that in all the newsletters I have sent out I have been telling people that we live in a place called Guanajuato, a small provincial capital somewhere in the mountains of central Mexico. "No one would ever want to go there; it's in the middle of nowhere." I told the delegation. The only way I would reveal the identity of our town would be through a secret code so difficult and impenetrable that no one from Wisconsin would ever crack it. "This will always remain our little secret," I said. "So what's your code name for this place?" I was asked. "It's **!ocixeM, anaujiT,**" I replied. They all agreed that no one from Wisconsin would ever be able to decipher the code and they all went home happy.

Battalón de San Patricio Postage Stamp

Readers of **Letter from Mexico** may notice a new postage stamp affixed to the cover page commemorating the 150th anniversary of the formation of the St. Patrick's Battalion. The battalion was composed of Irish immigrants who deserted the American Army to join Mexico during the 1847 Mexican-American War. When finally taken prisoner by U.S. forces, many were executed as deserters. Mexico honors the Irish on St. Patrick's Day for their help. Postage for a letter to Ireland, where this stamp might flatter the folks, is 5.20 pesos. The *San Patricio* stamp costs 3.40 pesos to the U.S. Would someone please tell Senator Fienstien to stop knocking Mexico so we don't have to endure subtle digs about this stamp.

Average Cumulative Income of Americans Living in San Miguel Plunges—Charities Expected to Suffer

Americans and Mexicans living in San Miguel de Allende were saddened to learn of the death of Mary Rockefeller, a part-time resident of the city. Mrs. Rockefeller, wife of, I believe, Laurence Rockefeller, died in her Manhattan apartment as the result of a fall. Mrs. Rockefeller was a generous donor to local charities in San Miguel.

Substantial Increase in Average Income of Americans in San Miguel is rumored—Charities May Benefit

Rumors are flying in San Miguel that Ted Turner and his wife, Jane Fonda Turner, are looking for a house to purchase in this city. Mr. Turner, who recently pledged one billion dollars to support various United Nations programs, is thought to still have another two bil. Recent fireworks display and dancing in the streets by San Miguellians were more likely due to Independence Day and not to the rumors of the Turner's arrival. People here are waiting for firmer confirmation before resuming dancing in the streets.

10

March 9, 1998

San Miguel Faces Ruin—Is Guanajuato Next? Traffic and Transportation, Eating Out in Guanajuato, Technology, Innovation and New Developments, Water

San Miguel Faces Ruin—Is Guanajuato Next?

A recent article in *Atención*, the English language newspaper of San Miguel, related some shocking news of what is happening to this beautiful little city that lies only fifty miles east of Guanajuato. The article contains extensive quotes from some of the top travel magazines published in the United States. The San Miguel paper tries desperately to put a favorable spin on this eminent calamity by failing to reveal the impending disaster. But urbanologists and city planning experts will be able to read between the lines and ascertain that the end is near for San Miguel. For those of us living in Guanajuato the big question is whether our town is next. *Letter from Mexico* quotes extensively from this December 22nd article written by Don Knoles of *Atención*:

1997: The Year San Miguell Rose To World's Top Travel Ranks

As confirmed by surveys by the two largest US travel magazines, San Miguel ascended to top ranks in ratings of the worlds best travel destinations. Hard to believe, but the two comprehensive polls indicate San Miguel is now more attractive to travelers than any other city in all of Latin America or the Orient and is topped in the US only by San Francisco, New Orleans, Chicago and the Hawaiian Islands. Many stops on Europe's grand tour now fall below San Miguel in the charts. *Condé Nast Traveler* touted its September survey of 36,929 readers as "the largest survey yet of consumer preferences in world travel." Astonishingly, San

Miguel was ranked number seven of the top twenty cities. Sydney was on top, followed by Rome, Florence, Venice, Paris, Vancouver, and then San Miguel. Lower down were cities such as London, and Vienna.

Rival magazine, *Travel and Leisure,* ranked San Miguel 17th among the world's top 25 cities. Mention of San Miguel in two other publications should also be noted. Last year, *Fortune Magazine* listed the city as one of the world's 20 best places to retire. And this past October, *Santa Fe* magazine, in a feature story, quoted New Mexico artists as saying San Miguell "captured their hearts" as Santa Fe had many years ago.

The article in *Atención* quoted a visiting artist who pointed out that one of the striking things about San Miguel is the large number of English-speaking expatriate Americans, Canadians and Europeans you notice when you are out walking. "Certainly," he concluded, "downtown real estate prices reflect the deeper pockets of these newcomers, with three-bedroom residences listed in the $300,000 (U.S.) range."

We, at **Letter from Mexico**, don't want to sound hysterical, **but don't these fools see what's happening! Is the significance of all this media attention only that real estate prices are going through the roof?**

There is a story going around these parts about the great Mexican comedian, Cantinflas, who was often called the Charlie Chaplin of Mexico. Cantinflas, while he was still living, had an elegant home in San Miguel, but he seldom stayed there. Someone once asked him why he never stayed in his beautiful home in San Miguel. Cantinflas replied, "I can't stay there, I don spik Engleesh so gooed."

Many cities in the State of Guanajuato have at their entrance a monument emblematic of that city. For example, Leon, which claims to be the center of shoe manufacturing in North America, has at its main highway entrance, a bronze statue of an old cobbler making a pair of shoes. Moroleon, another town in our state, is famous for its textiles. At the entrance to the town stand three twenty-foot high spools of what looks like brightly colored thread. Guanajuato, which prides itself on its long history as a center of mining, has at its principle entrance a large bronze statue of two miners driving a wedge into rock. And at the other end of town, at the *Embajadoras,* there is a statue commemorating Guanajuato's contribution to World War II. The monument consists of two figures, a soldier holding his M-1 rifle and a miner holding a pneumatic hammer. It occurred to me that while San Miguel de Allende has various statues of heroic figures who played important roles in Mexico's and San Miguell's history, they don't have a single statue depicting the principal activity that defines the place today. I have a suggestion for San Miguel. They should erect a bigger than life bronze statue of an old guy with his camera and a little old lady with her easel and paintbrushes.

*Editor's note to our good friends in San Miguel: You know that we are just kidding. All of us here in Guanajuato are proud of the recognition bestowed on your town by these American publications. I think everyone realizes that San Miguel will **always** be a very special place and remain tops among the panoply of quintessentially Mexican cities. Those of us who live in Guanajuato know that when we want Sushi, or fresh bagels, we have to go to San Miguel.*

Traffic and Transportation, Guanajuato Style

There's a certain flair to the way Mexicans initiate a new undertaking. This came home to me one day when we were driving past the *Embajadoras* Park. Carole called out to me, "Look at that! A new push cart stand and they have a banner announcing: *Gran Inauguración*." The shiny new pushcart located under a huge shade tree serves up seafood cocktails to as many as four customers at a time. The owner of this stand was announcing a grand opening and offering special low prices for this tasty fare to introduce his new eatery to the public.

A few days later, the local newspapers announced another *Gran Inaugurción*, only this time it was to mark the start of construction of the new *entrada,* a new entrance to the city. I have attended my share of public works project openings and they tend to follow a similar pattern. Several senior elected officials try to stomp a chrome plated shovel into the ground. This is known as the ground breaking. Surrounding them is a bunch of beaming contractors all wearing construction hard hats. I'm not sure why hard hats are necessary unless they think the old guys with the chrome plated shovels might get a little wild and start swinging the shovels at 'em. But in Guanajuato they do it with style. The governor recently participated in the *gran inaugurición* by setting off a dynamite charge with one of those plungers we used to see in old cowboy movies. The project here is like no other highway improvement project I have known. The *entrada* includes two sections of tunnel and a highway bridge made of cut stone with arches to match the Spanish colonial era bridges and aqueducts that grace Guanajuato.

To understand the need for this project you should have some idea of the unique physiographic setting of Guanajuato and the highway system that serves it. The city is built along the slopes of a winding canyon. Basically, there are only two roads that enter or leave the city. One on the northeast comes from Dolores

Hidalgo, and one on the south is joined by three other highways that feed into it from various towns south and east of here. Arriving from any other direction is precluded by the Sierra Guanajuato Mountains. One of these three roads is a modern four lane divided freeway which with the other roads all feed into a winding two-lane highway which takes you to the center of Guanajuato. As you can imagine this main entrance to Guanajuato is frequently congested. The Mexican traffic engineers in Guanajuato have done a marvelous job of dealing with traffic through the use of traffic circles, called *glorietas,* channelization, speed bumps and *vibradoras* that rumble your car sufficiently to cause you to slow down. Guanajuato doesn't have a single traffic signal although they are common even in small towns in Mexico. Traffic police control the critical intersections. Most of these police officers are trim and agile which is exactly what is needed given the narrowness of the streets. Before I understood the system, I found their whistle blowing annoying. I thought that when a policeman blows his whistle at you it means stop. Apparently here, it means keep moving, or hurry up.

The new entrance project is designed to relieve congestion on this two-lane road. The project added a thoroughfare that cuts through the hills and is parallel with the old highway. The project was announced in October and construction began January. It is scheduled to be finished in September of this year. This seems incredibly fast for a project such as this but they seem to be quite adept at building tunnels and doing stonework and not having any public hearings is a real time saver.

A few weeks ago, one of our neighbors called and said that an engineer from the tunnel project stopped at each house in our neighborhood to inform us of the impending blasting. Because we were not at home at the time, our neighbor was asked to relate this information. I would have liked to hear just exactly how they stated this. Here's the way I imagine it:

"Ahem! We're building this tunnel through your neighborhood and some segments will be about six hundred feet from your house. There is a certain amount of blasting that will be necessary but you have nothing to worry about in as much as the tunnel is not directly under your residence. Yes, it's true that with the last tunnel we built in Guanajuato, there were a couple of houses that slipped down a tad, but that's why this tunnel avoids any houses. Most of the blasting will take place at night. There are two reasons for this. First, it doesn't make much difference to tunnel workers if it's night or day. Second, we really prefer to deliver and unload the dynamite at night when traffic is lighter on Guanajuato's congested streets; after all, getting rid of congestion is why we're building this tunnel, isn't it? Oh, and by the way, it's probably best if you don't come home too late at night."

Well, I never heard the explanation, but a few nights later, Carole had gone to bed and I had dozed off in front of the TV. I awoke with a start when I heard this enormous WHOOMPF, followed by what sounded like a super sonic jet plane, only under the ground, and passing directly below me. I suppose this was a shock wave radiating away from the epicenter of the blast. Just about every night since, we hear the blasting. Sometimes it comes in the form of a rapid series of blasts, WHOOMPF, WHOOMPF, WHOOMPF, WHOOMPF. There is no way to describe it except that you seem to feel it in your belly as much as hear it in your ears. By now, we have become accustomed to this noise, and it scarcely wakes us up, except as happened last night, when there were about ten WHOOMPFs in rapid succession, more than we had ever heard. Carole woke up and said, "What was that?" Somehow, I hope they can settle down to a more consistent pattern of WHOOMPFing.

I want to inject a personal note to members of our family, friends and our insurance agent. We don't feel that there really is any danger to us or to our house, although last Friday they blew out our phone and water service. All was back in order three days later. However, if any of you happen to have one of those old World War I army helmets, I wish you would send it to us. I think Carole would look cute in one of those tin helmets carrying a flashlight.

Eating Out in Guanajuato

For some weeks now I've been toying around with the idea and talking with some friends about putting together a guide book on Guanajuato—a real insiders guide to the city. In a previous addition of *Letter from Mexico*, I mentioned how all the writers of tourist guides on this place failed to mention the pretty girls here. Anyone this unobservant is likely to miss a lot of other things too and so perhaps we could put together a guidebook that was both useful and engaging. Guanajuato is peculiar in a number of ways. For example, while there are at least four airlines with international flights that serve the Leon/Guanajuato airport, plus several other national airlines with flights to other cities in the country, only one airline has deigned it necessary to list its telephone number in the phone directory. On the other hand, the Otis Elevator Company has a listing and even a display ad in the yellow pages, although to the best of my knowledge, there are only two elevators in the entire town. One is at the University, and requires prior approval for its use and the other is an antique lift in The Hotel San Diego, which is operated by a bellhop, or as they say in Spanish, *butones,* or 'buttons', from the brass fasteners traditional with uniforms of persons in this calling. A visitor to our town who still remembers some of the Spanish they learned in school and who wants to contact an airline, might think of looking under the V's in the phone book, for *'viaje',* which means travel, as in travel agency, figuring that travel agencies would know airline phone numbers. This is good thinking except he wouldn't find anything under the V's. He would have to look under the A's, for *agencia,* agency and there find *Agencias de Viajes.* What I'm trying to convey is one could use a little help in dealing with this town.

The guide book, which is in progress but may never get finished, includes restaurants, stores and services of all kinds, a list of the things we think are most fun to do in Guanajuato, things for kids to do and even includes a guide to street beggars, after all you want your peso to go as far as possible when you visit Mexico. A special and I believe useful feature, which I don't think you would find in the typical guidebook, is a toilet rating for restaurants indicated by toilet bowl icons. Five lids up indicate the cleanest, finest restrooms in town. One lid up indicates that there probably is no toilet seat let alone a lid. We all like clean and modern restrooms and as far as we know we are the only Guanajuato guidebook that includes this vital information. But, for those who simply can't put up with Guanajuato style toilet facilities, we recommend a visit to the Kohler museum in Kohler Wisconsin where you may see and enjoy the most splendiferous johns in the world, but alas, there won't be any *mariachi* music wafting in through the window.

We have provided street addresses and directions for finding the places we have mentioned in this guidebook. However, given the irregularity and complexity of the street system, residents as well as visitors may encounter difficulty in finding some of the places mentioned. Often as you traverse a street, the street name will change several times or even the same block may have two different names, one being an older name that was never removed from the corner of a building. But as a further aid for locating places, we have included map coordinates for each establishment using the *GUIA ROJA* map, which in our opinion is the best map of this city even though it is a bit dated. You won't find the street we live on either although it has been around for at least eight years. Here is a sampling from the Gringo's Guide to Guanajuato:

Restaurants, *Zona Centro*

Guanajuato is not noted for having a lot of fine restaurants; the best cooking is in the homes of people who live here. Some of us think the food prepared with substantial help of Mexican cooks in our homes is simply some of the most delicious food we have ever eaten. Even if you are not on anyone's dinner guest list, we hope *The Gringo's Guide* can be of help to you in identifying enjoyable places to eat.

Santa Fe Restaurant [G5]—Located in front of the Hotel Santa Fe on the Jardin Union. This outdoor restaurant is one of the most enjoyable places to eat in town because of its location, its high quality offerings and its service. Prices are a little higher than other places. After your meal, enjoy a cappuccino and watch the pretty girls and handsome young guys walk by, which we feel, more than makes up for the lack of five star quality restaurants here. Inside the hotel you will find large paintings depicting various legends of Guanajuato. Written explanations of these legends appear in the corner of the painting written in Olde Spanish script. For persons not adept at modern Spanish let alone Olde Spaniſh, our advice to you is juſt look at the pictureſ. Restrooms rate four lids up.

Valadez Restaurant [G5]—Located across the street from the Teatro Juarez and on the corner of the Jardin Union. This restaurant serves typical Mexican dishes. We would rate the food as good but not great. Some very fancy deserts are served here. The place is spick and span clean. Water if requested with a meal is purified with equipment in the restaurant and is not the purified water sold by the bottle. It's probably O.K. but you may want to order commercially bottled water, a soft drink or any one of a number of excellent Mexican beers. Sometimes the restaurant features a keyboard artist who plays a lot of American standards, plenty loud so it's not necessary to talk a lot. Some of us would prefer an unamplified guitarist playing the romantic music of Mexico. Decor looks to us like a Mexican restaurant designer's idea of a nice American restaurant. Noisy. Prices are moderate. Four lids up.

Picachos Restaurant [G5]—Located at 22 Calle Contarranas (Singing Frogs Street) two doors to the right of the Teatro Principal. Even though it is in the heart of town, you probably won't find this restaurant. First of all it has no sign identifying it as a restaurant. Second, it is closed every Monday, Tuesday and Wednesday of each week while the owner drives to Tepic, Nyarit on the Pacific coast to pick up fresh fish. And also they close it when they run out of fish. You can tell when the restaurant is open for business because the door, which is about eight feet wide and twelve feet tall is swung open. In times past this door probably accommodated horse drawn coaches with baggage and riders on top. Peek in and near the entrance you will see a glass display case with fish and seafood on ice. The restaurant occupies the central patio courtyard of an old building. With some money this could be a pretty place, but as it stands now, it is not particularly distinctive. We heard about the marvelous fish served at Picachos from Charles and Pamela Towill, a couple of Brits who split their year between their homes in Alaska and here in Guanajuato. We recieved identical yet independent reviews from Dr. John and Mercedes Lichtwardt who split their year between their homes in Michigan and Guanajuato. What with the salmon in Alaska and the Walleyes in Michigan these folks probably know fish better than Mrs. Paul. Both gave rave reviews on the *Robólo*, which is sea bass from the Pacific. The fish is first brought to your table from the ice display case in its uncooked form. After your inspection the waiter takes it to one side of the patio to a large charcoal grill where Julian, the owner, dresses it with a special *salsa estylo Nyarit.* Splayed open, the fish is cooked until it is lightly and gorgeously charred. Everyone agreed it was the best fish they had ever eaten. When five of us ate at Picachos, the grilled fish, probably about 28 inches head to tail, was served whole at our table on a platter. Each of us was given a plate with some rice on it and a fork. We didn't quite know how to make servings with only a fork so we asked for a knife. The waiter returned with a knife that looked like one of those serrated bread knives. Ron Mann, one of our dinner companions, deftly divided the fish into servings for each of us. Ron is a splendid cook; not just concerned with how food tastes but also with its presentation. At Picachos, he didn't say anything about the presentation of the *róbolo*. He just dug in like the rest of us. And as for me, well I never checked out the rest rooms. When it's this good, who cares?

Technology, Innovation and New Developments

When one thinks of technology and innovation, I think it's fair to say; one is not likely to think of Mexico. But I continue to be surprised by many things I learn about this country. A couple of months ago I was reading a book about the history of Mexico's many revolutionary battles and was surprised to learn that the first aerial bombardment in the history of warfare occurred in Mexico. I was also surprised to learn that the foxhole was invented in Mexico. This made trench warfare obsolete. General Obregon, who later became president of this country, is credited with this invention. The word for fox in Spanish is zorro. And I can imagine the general saying to his troops, "I'm going to make a mark on the ground and I want all of you to make like zorro." The rest is history and the real mark of zorro is not some fancy sword work but a hole in the ground. But I digress.

In a recent article in the Manchester Guardian Weekly, I read an interesting report concerning Mexico City. As we all know, Mexico City is one of the largest cities in the world. Twenty million people live in this metropolis, more people than live in Canada. Although I would prefer not to live in a city such as this there must be something very special about these mega-conurbations that continue to grow in spite of their awesome size. Aren't people voting with their feet when they keep moving into a place like Mexico City, Tokyo or Madison, Wisconsin for that matter? One of the awful consequences of this enormous growth in Mexico City is pollution, particularly air pollution. It is often reported that Mexico City is the most polluted large city in the world. Part of this is due to the natural setting of the city. The city is built on an old lakebed and air is trapped within this intermountain basin. Although we have not driven there we've read about the heavy duty measures the city is taking in regulating the use of private autos on certain days of the week. Here in the State of Guanajuato, we are required to have a vehicle inspection every six months. Our car gets hooked up to a device that is controlled by a computer and it checks vehicle emissions. The Guardian reported that a French engineer has invented an urban car that runs only on the air around us. The first ZP taxi—the ZP stands for zero pollution—was scheduled to be unveiled February in France before it goes into mass production in Mexico. The inventor perfected a motor that runs on a tankful of compressed air. In urban road tests his CitroenAX chassis ran for ten hours with a top speed of 62 mph. This is better performance than any electric car in production.

The Mexican version of the vehicle was designed by an Italian company and resembles a small family sedan, with a separate compartment for the driver and four seats in the back. A Mexican government licensee has signed a contract to produce 40,000 ZP taxis and urban delivery vehicles per year. It hopes to replace all of Mexico City's 87,000 gasoline and diesel taxis. The inventor, Guy Negre, worked on high performance and Formula One engines for 30 years, and runs his business with his son, who is a former Bughatti engineer. His silent and odor free engine design was chosen by Mexican authorities after they tested dozens of electric and other non-polluting experimental vehicles. Three hundred liters of compressed air can be pumped into the tank under high pressure in three minutes. The car can be refueled at home in four hours by a small compressor in the car linked to the house electric supply. While the air is free, the electricity used to fuel the tank at home would cost less than $2. In contrast, about half the energy put into a battery of an electric car never comes out again. It can attain speeds of up to 62 mph. That's not real fast, but should be fast enough for cities. The car takes in air as it brakes, and has a carbon block filtration system, so the air that it exhausts is actually cleaner than the air that comes in—a car that cleans the air!

Closer to home, the newspapers have reported a proposal to build a rapid transit system that will initially connect the City of Leon with Silao, Irapuato, Celaya, and with a branch from Silao to the City of Guanajuato, all in the State of Guanajuato. The trains are to be built by the Bombardier Company in Canada and the financing will largely be from private Canadian sources. The cost is estimated at 800 million U.S. dollars. The cost of a ticket will be about the same as a first class bus ticket. The trains will go sixty miles an hour and will use existing intercity bus terminals along its route. After thirty years the system will be turned over to the State of Guanajuato.

While I believe the story about the compressed air car to be built in Mexico, and the one about the first aerial bombardment, and even the one about the invention of the foxhole, I just can't believe the reports on this privately financed rapid transit system. I would like to think this is going to happen but it just doesn't seem financially feasible. No mention is made of extending the system to Guadalajara or Queretero, two large cites in neighboring states or to Mexico City, which would give this system some real traffic volume. Yet, this project has been reported rather matter-of-factly several times in various newspapers.

Another recent report is that the Hilton Hotel Corporation is going to build a $10,000,000 hotel complex in Guanajuato. This includes shops and a golf course. In the financial pages of a Mexico City newspaper, Hilton announced that they were going to build twenty hotels in Mexico so maybe it's true that Guanajuato is on their list. I would be interested in knowing where they intend to get the water for the golf coarse. Maybe they could bring it in on the rail rapid transit from some other town that has decided it would like to die of thirst.

Water

As a boy growing up in Janesville, Wisconsin, I will never forget the hot humid summers that we endured. Long continuing heat waves would eventually be brought to an end by thundershowers. The local newspaper would carry front-page headlines: **"Million Dollar Rain Saves Corn Crop."** The same headline and the same story would appear year after year. This was way back in the 1930's and 40's when journalists wouldn't think of writing a story with unattributable sources or of using leaks even for a story about rain. The reporter would of course seek out the most authoratative source for this front-page story. Not being able to talk directly with God, he would naturally interview the next best source—the local county extension agent. For years and years I was always perplexed as to how the county agent came up with the million-dollar estimate. More mysterious to me was that the value of these rain events never increased—always one million dollars. I first started to notice these headlines when you could still buy a hot dog for a nickel and see a double feature movie for a dime. We all know what a movie costs today but crop saving rains are still going for an even million dollars. Perhaps this explains why so many farmers quit farming. The cost of everything went up but the value of the rains remained constant.

In my career as a Dane County (Wisconsin) regional planner I had the opportunity of getting to know Bill Clark, the county agent. One day I asked Bill about those million dollar rain stories and he admitted that they didn't really have a way of evaluating the dollar benefit of these rains—they sort of made it up. I think they knew that reporters would stop coming around if they proclaimed that the county had an eight hundred and ninety seven thousand four hundred and sixty five-dollar rain.

Now that I know how they come up with these estimates I feel confident enough to proclaim in **Letter from Mexico,** "**Guanajuato Receives Million Peso Rain!**" The problem is I'm still waiting for the event. In the last two months, or is it five, we have barely had a trace of rain. Cuco, our part time gardener, squirts a few inches of water in my bone-dry rain gage just to shake me up. You know how it is when the first snowfall comes in the north and those soft snowflakes hit the warm ground and immediately melt. A similar thing occurs when raindrops hit pavement in ultra dry periods in this ultra dry town. The water simply evaporates when it hits the pavement. Step out into this rain and you can feel some moisture hitting your face and arms but the pavement remains dry. Of course we need the rain but I have to admit that I love the sunny skys, the crisp air, and the lack of mosquitoes and flies.

11

June 1998

Courtesy and Politeness, Lessons We Can Learn from the Spanish Inquisition, Big Problem for Mexico, Better than a Margarita, New Computer

Courtesy and Politeness

"As courteous as a Mexican Indian" was a Spanish saying as early as 1550, according to English historian Hugh Thomas. "In good manners, I dare say the Mexicans were then as now the superior to most of whom they came in contact."

One of the things noticeable to us in Guanajuato is the great courtesy and politeness people display toward us as well as to each other. When we meet a Mexican couple on the street that we know, and even some that we don't know, they stop and warmly greet us: "*Buenos dias,*" they say. "*Buenos dias,*" we respond. Then we shake hands. If we are one couple meeting another couple there are four handshakes, each person from one couple shaking hands with each of the other couple. But if two couples meet two couples, this gets a little out of hand—there can be sixteen handshakes. Everyone enquires about the other couple's children and is asked to convey their salutations to family members not present. As you can imagine this takes quite a bit of time. It's not good form to rush this ritual even if you are in a hurry to make an appointment or are dying to go to the bathroom.

What I have described is a generalized and simplified version of these encounters. In actuality, men lightly buss women on the cheek, women buss women on the cheek, and everyone shakes hands. In certain situations, men will give each other a great big hug, *abrazo*. This actually happened to me at Christmas time when I gave my barber 50 pesos (about six dollars) for a haircut and a beard trim, instead of the more customary 25 pesos. For 100 pesos maybe I might have been kissed: I don't know. But there is more. After the initial round of hand shaking, hugging and kissing, and a round of polite enquiries about children and the weather, there is a **second** round of handshaking, and kissing at the time of departure. If there should be a baby in the group, figure on a lot more time for ooh-ing and ah-ing.

This is only one small example of the courtesy and politeness one encounters in Guanajuato. Walk into a clothing store in our town and ask where you can find some chicken wire for your rose plants and the owner or clerk will usually walk out into the street with you and point out the directions to help you find the hardware store. Phone conversations cannot really begin until there is a full discussion of how you are, even though in ten out of ten cases you are fine, or if you actually were sick you would just as soon keep it to yourself.

In previous issues of *Letter from Mexico* I have been critical of governmental bureaucracy in this country. And while I believe that government and big business are laden with a bureaucratic tradition of enormous proportions, the basic politeness of the Mexican often shines through. On more than one occasion when I have gone to the post office only to find it closed for some obscure holiday, a postal worker seeing me through the glass doors will unlock the building so that I can get to my postal box. On some occasions the postal clerk has even helped me affix the postage stamps on the letters I am sending.

Just today I saw the head of the Water Commission in our big supermarket. We have been having a terrible problem with the water pressure at the house. Some days it is just fine and other days our pipes vibrate and howl, apparently from excessive water pressure. We have tried all sorts of fixes, such as air chambers to cushion the high pressure, but nothing has worked. For some time I have thought it might be a good idea to check with the Water Commission. Perhaps they were familiar with this problem and knew what to do. All of the plumbers I spoke to about this didn't think much of the idea of asking the people at the water works. Mexicans have a very poor regard for their government. Well, when I saw the Commissioner at the grocery store, I went over to him and said, "Excuse me sir, I have this problem with our water pressure." The Commissioner greeted me warmly and said what I need was a water pressure valve. "Come with me, he said, "we will go to the Commission offices and I will help you get signed up for a special valve that should take care of the problem; workers will be at your house tomorrow." I protested that I didn't want to bother him with this. (The verb in Spanish for this is "*molestar,*" but I don't think it's quite the same as "molest" in English, at least I hope not.) The Commissioner runs a large and important organization; there are at least sixteen reservoirs and a complex water distribution system. He walked me to the office and helped me with the valve order.

These displays of courtesy can probably be put down as charming Mexican folkways for anthropologists to record and tourists to witness, somewhat like watching folk dancing. Although all this courtesy is nice and I wouldn't want to eliminate it, there is a big problem with much of this. This politeness takes an enormous amount of time, and what's more, it is contagious. The foreigners who live here, man, woman, and child are all exceedingly polite just like the Mexicans.

Let me illustrate with an incident that happened to us a few weeks ago. Carole and I had signed up for a visit organized by the Rainbow Connection, which is a group of Mexican and American women she belongs to that raises money to help kids. One of their fund-raising efforts was to organize a visit to Lagos de Moreno, which is a town in the northwestern part of the state. It is not a large town, but it has an enormous and very beautiful church and some old colonial mansions we visited. The town is exceptionally clean and neat. In the central part of city there is a certain air of elegance. The architectural historian who served as our guide explained that the Spanish who were ferociously opposed by the Chichimeca Indians settled the town in the mid 1500's. The walls of the early convent we visited were thick enough to have withstood a cannon bombardment. Eventually, the Spanish won, but not without a struggle. Our guide mentioned that in the early days, at a time when the entire Kingdom of New Spain had about 400 *hidalgos,* noblemen, Lagos de Moreno with a population of only 9,000 inhabitants, had eighty of these Spanish aristocrats. And then, with a laugh, he added, that's why people from other parts of Mexico consider those of us from Lagos, as being snooty. He pushed up his nose with a finger, turned his head to the side, and offered us a profile view.

On the morning of the trip as we were getting ready, Carole said to me that she wasn't feeling well but she thought but that she would start to feel better later and wanted to go. For a while she felt O.K. but by lunchtime she told me she was feeling worse, wanted to skip the meal, and go outside for some air. People in our group noticed that she had left the dining room and everyone was most solicitous and asked me how she was feeling and could they help. Thinking that I could find something to settle her stomach, I asked our tour leader where there was a pharmacy and she said, "Oh, poor Carole, we have a doctor in our group, and grabbing me by the hand, said, "Come with me, Charlie, come with me. I knew we had a physician in our group. Dr. Lichtwardt and his wife Merc are friends of ours, but I didn't think Carole wanted to see a proctologist, or is he a urologist? All Carole wanted was a little air.

I joined Carole as she sat in the shade on a stone step in front of a building opposite the restaurant holding her head with both hands. Two policemen drove by on their motorcycles, both giving us a nice smile and a polite salute. I felt as if we were on a reviewing stand for a police parade. Other folks stepped around us with the usual cordialities for this time of day. I thought Carole would be more comfortable and not require folks to step over her legs if we could make it over to the handsome plaza facing the big church. The plaza has heavy shade and the typical cast iron park benches typical of Mexico that make quite an impression when you sit down on them for long. The two of us ambled over to the plaza, where Carole was able to sit down more normally but still hold on to her head. I don't want to be too explicit but Carole said she didn't want anything, except perhaps if I could find her a plastic bag. I started to walk to the nearby stores to pick up a bag but most of the establishments were closed, it being the hour for Lagosians to eat and take their siestas. Here I am, looking for a barf bag, and I keep running into all the tour people who by this time had left the restaurant and were wandering all over the center of town looking for more historical sites. I don't know if they thought I had abandoned Carole and was just out sightseeing, or that I had lost her, but they kept telling me that my wife was in the park and could they be of help. The attention and solicitude continued on the bus ride back to Guanajuato and for several days after. All of this concern made me wonder if I had misjudged the magnitude of Carole's condition and whether we would be losing her soon. It seems that a better part of one's life here is spent being polite.

I have decided as a person from the upper mid-west, and more particularly from Wisconsin, I am uniquely qualified to straighten Mexico out on this business of courtesy and politeness. When my courtesy management plan (CMP) takes hold, Mexico will be able to compete under NAFTA with the best that New York City, Los Angeles and Chicago have to offer. Where I come from, people have been able to reduce the expression. "Yes, you are certainly most welcome," to a shorter and less time-consuming, "Yah, you betcha!" People in Wisconsin are probably just as nice as other people, they just happen to be more direct.

What I am proposing under CMP is a more efficient way of being polite. A numerical code would replace phrases like *Buenos dias, Buenos tardes,* or *Buenos notches.* These could be expressed as #3, #4, and #5. (I thought in the interest of not confusing small children that we would reserve #1 and #2 for other expressions.) Each standard greeting would be given a code; #10 could be *"adios"* for example.

Instead of using so much time shaking hands, which as I pointed out takes place when people meet and when they part, people could all put their hands forward on top of each other the way football players do before the kickoff, and make one big shaking motion.

Now as to the time spent kissing and hugging, under CMP, this can be reduced substantially without eliminating this fine custom. The youngest, loveliest, grown up female in the group would pucker up to be kissed by, let's say, one of the older shorter men. Let's say, by one of the more witty men, as judged by his ability to make puns, or by other similar scientific methods of determining urbanity and erudition. The young woman representing youth and feminine beauty would be kissed by the old man exemplifying intelligence and wisdom, thus representing all who are present and thereby, symbolically involving all of them in this display of courtesy.

O.K., Mexico, let's get started. #10.

(Note: After publishing this article in my newsletter I received an email from Ted Murray of Tulsa,Oklahoma saying that he liked the article especially the part where the pretty girl kisses the old fart.)

Lessons We Can Learn from the Spanish Inquisition

On visits to San Miguel de Allende one can hardly avoid seeing the building where the work of the Spanish Inquisition took place. It's a rather plain building near the center of town, marked by a stone cross of a rather unusual design above the door. Across the street is a handsome building known as the House of the Inquisitor, which served as the residence. For some time I have been interested in the Inquisition, an institution right out of the middle ages, for the lessons it can teach us today. The Spanish version of the Inquisition didn't really get started until after 200 years of development in other parts of Europe, but once established in Spain lasted for 300 years and extended throughout Latin America.

Until recently I have not been able to find a similar set of buildings in Guanajuato as the ones in San Miguel. Not long ago, however, I discovered where the Inquisition was held in this town. The building is not as well marked as the one in San Miguel, but it is a lot bigger. It's a three story building located on the Plaza de la Paz directly facing the Basilica, and, if you pardon the expression, just a stones' throw away. Many times as I approached this building at night I could hear screams emanating from this building where for so many years the Inquisitor General did his work. Actually, today the place is a restaurant with a disco upstairs, which probably accounts for most of the noise. The current function of disco is what city planners would regard as a creative example of a re-adaptive use for a house of torture.

It seems to me that any institution that lasted three hundred years night be worth examining. Yes, yes, I know that today the Inquisition is generally regarded as belonging to the darker side of Christian history, but given that it lasted as long as it did, can't we learn from this experience? For example, Tomas Torquemada, first of the special prosecutors of the Spanish Inquisition, is almost universally reviled as a symbol of poor judgment and fanaticism—sort of an early day Kenneth Starr. But in truth, Torquemada was like Joe Friday—all he wanted were the facts. He operated under the law, using standard prosecutorial techniques of squeezing his witnesses and targets. Squeezing worked then as it does today, just ask Monica, but why did Toquemada end up with such a bad image. Modern historians have established that a lot more were burned at the stake in England, Germany, Italy and France than under the Spanish Inquisition, so why all the bad press for Torqui and his successors? The answer is that Torquemada didn't have his own PR staff. He let the English tell the world—big mistake. English spin-doctors gave us the version we are familiar with today. Thus grew the infamous "Black Legend" and tales of the Spanish Inquisition. English spin-doctors of the day described the Spanish in such vile terms that hardly anyone today wants to defend the Spanish Inquisition, in spite of its efficiency, greater attention to legal procedures and to law and order.

Big Problem for Mexico

It seems that if you read American newspapers all you ever hear about Mexico is its problems. From here it seems a little unbalanced but let's face it, Mexico has a lot of problems. And while I don't like to harp on the negative, there is one problem that I believe needs to be addressed. You don't hear a lot about this problem in the American press but the problem of guns being smuggled across the border is becoming a concern, especially for ex-pats like us. Guanajuato tends to be fifty to a hundred years behind times so fortunately the gun problem hasn't reached us yet. Right now there is only one store in Guanajuato where you can buy a gun and that's at the Commercial Mexicana. Four years ago there were no stores that sold guns. This is our big supermarket, part of a chain of stores that sells groceries and dry goods. I've been watching their gun marketing effort for some time now and have never seen a gun sold, or for that matter seen a customer even look at the weapons in the case. The locked wood and glass cabinet that holds the guns has been moved to different parts of the store, I suppose to a spot that would be conducive to some sales. First, it was next to men's clothing, then the hardware department, and then to the liquor store. As yet, they haven't moved the gun case next to the little branch bank within the store, although that might give somebody an idea for buying a gun. The locked case has three rifles consisting of two

.22 caliber weapons, and one .17 caliber gun, the later I suppose is used to hunt mice.

It's O.K. with me that most ordinary people don't have or don't carry guns in Guanajuato. The police have them, the security guards have them and on a couple of occasions I have seen the Mexican Army pass through here and they have them. The other day the engineer that designed the electrical wiring for our house came for a visit. He showed me a picture of a pair of antique pistols that he said belonged to a friend. He was inquiring as to whether these pistols could be advertised on the Internet. He had a description of these guns clipped out of some American publications. I don't remember if it was the *American Rifleman*, the *American Serial Killer*, or *Shooting for Fun and Profit*, but the description said these pistols were used by the American Army in the 1840's. In 1846 President Polk moved against Mexico and took half of its territory, but in all probability not without the loss of these pistols. Now they can be repatriated. The problem in other parts of Mexico, such as Mexico City, Guadalajara, and along the U.S. border is quite a different thing. I read recently that there are certain streets in Mexico City where you can buy almost any kind of handgun made in the world. Some of these weapons come from the rogue country of Iraq, some from the rogue country of China, but most of the weapons come from the non-rogue country of the United States. The problem is serious enough that the Mexican Senate recently passed a law increasing the penalty for bringing guns into Mexico to a sentence of thirty years.

I would think Mexico would want to consider more effective means of controlling the illegal importation of weapons into Mexico. They could, for example set up a certification process that requires the president of Mexico to annually certify that each country that is the source of these illegal arms is doing all it can to control the entry of guns into Mexico. The trouble with this idea is that Americans might think that Mexico is overreaching a bit. The nerve of those Mexicans telling **us** what **we** should do to solve **their** problem. If the Mexicans have a problem with people buying guns and shooting up, why don't they just stop buying them?

Another measure idea would be to build a wall along the 1,200-mile border that separates our two countries. This shouldn't be too hard to do, after all the US has managed to complete sixty and one-quarter miles; Mexico only needs to complete an additional twelve hundred thirty-seven and three-quarter more miles to finish the job. An article in the *New York Times* described the border barrier (It is not to be called a wall.) that the United States recently completed in Nogales Arizona. It's one-quarter of a mile long and cost $750,000, which works out to

$3,000,000 per mile, and it represented something of a challenge to the design-
ers. The specifications included. "The barrier must be resistant to repeated physical assault by means such as welding torches, chisels, hammers, firearms, climbing
over or penetration with vehicles." And one thing else the government said,
"Make the barrier absolutely as friendly looking as possible, something that will
evoke the friendship between the two nations." I don't know if Mexico is capable
of producing a design as pleasing as the one in Arizona, but if Mexico can finish
the job at the same rate and cost that the US incurred in Nogales, it will take 569
years and cost three billion four hundred million dollars. There still might be a
problem with this project. Until the barrier is completed in the year 2567, people
might just walk around the unfinished ends with their guns. Let's check this out
with Pat Buchanan.

Perhaps there is another way. Maybe Mexico could send its Federal agents
across the international border and simply kidnap the gun lords. It's been tried
before when the US sent its undercover agents to kidnap and return to the US
someone we wanted in the war on drugs. Now to give a raid like this a little piz-
zazz, they could send a special unit of the Mexican army to California. Let me
explain. You know how the American army has a special bagpipe band dressed in
kilts, and a special drum and fife unit dressed in tri-corner hats and red coats, no
less. (I guess the idea is for every army to honor ancient foes by adopting some of
their more colorful uniform styles.) Well the Mexican army has one of the most
incredible cavalry units imaginable. The soldiers are decked out in Roman armor
and carry Roman short swords. This might seem a bit ludicrous to you until you
see them riding their horses, actually standing on them bareback, at full gallop
flailing away with their swords. I actually saw this on TV once as a part of an
armed forces day event and was quite amazed—first at their superlative riding
skills, and second at their sturdy legs and undies, revealed by the skirt like leather
armor that tended to flap up as they rode by. Now try to imagine this picture.
What if this special unit entered the US one day and arrived at Charlton Heston's
place. As a leading spokesman for gun-lords, Heston would certainly be an
appropriate abductee. I suppose Charlton would hop on one of his old chariots,
but I don't think he would be any match for this cavalry unit. I can hear him yell-
ing; "Mr. Zedillo, tear down that wall, or, guns don't kill people, people kill people, especially if they carry Roman swords!" Actually, Heston would be spirited
away to Mexico for a fair trial. He would be defended by experienced American
legal counsel, let's say the attorney that defended Manuel Noriega of Panama and
managed to get him put away for a long time. Fortunately for Heston, Mexico
doesn't have capital punishment, although there is an ancient tradition of shoot-

ing people who attempt to escape incarceration. Charlton, don't be fooled by any unlocked doors in your prison.

Better than a Margarita

I read in *Newsweek* some time ago that the Margarita has become the most popular mixed drink served in America. It's a good drink as long as the proportions are right and there is enough ice—but please don't make it into a snow cone. I have observed that some American bars are making Margaritas without any tequila, substituting brandy. That is pathetic. Here is my idea of a perfect margarita.

Margarita

2 oz. lime juice (4 little Mexican limes, probably 1 ½ big American limes)

3 oz. Tequila

3 oz. Triple Sec

2 cups of ice cubes

Put ingredients in blender and blend until ice turns into chips. Rim two glasses lightly with a cut piece of lime, invert glasses in dish of salt, and shake loose salt from glasses. Pour mixture, garnish with piece of lime. Serves two. *Es perfecto!*

A kinder, gentler drink than a margarita and one that is very easy to make is a La Paloma.

La Paloma (The Dove)

Take a tall glass, rim and salt the top as with the margarita. Fill the glass with ice cubes, pour a generous jigger of tequila, squeeze half a lime and fill the glass with Squirt. If you can't find Squirt, use Fresca, almost as good. *Es mu bueno!*

The next drink is called *Un Bul.* When you come to Guanajuato and order "A Bull", the waiter will look perplexed and say they don't make it. Try again and say you want, "Un Boool!" "Boool" is pronounced emphatically, almost explosively. This, in my opinion, is a wonderful summer cooler. I was first served this drink at a farewell party put on by Ron Mann, Sandra Ward, and Betsy McNair, *chef extraordinaire*/caterer and manager of the most unusual bed and breakfast, *Casa de Espiritus Alegre.* The party was given in one of the two courtyards of the *Ex Hacienda de la Trinidad.* Rocendo and Carlene Guitierez, an American Architect and his wife, who own the house, are from New Mexico. Rocendo has fig-ured out how to carry out his architectural practice in the US as well as Mexico through the Internet. When we entered the courtyard where the party was being held, Ron, who had previously visited this place, said to me that this was one of the most beautiful houses in Mexico. Rocendo later explained to me that there were many of these *ex-haciendas* that were available a few decades ago, if you were willing to repair the extensive damage from the disastrous flood of 1905 and the neglect that followed abandonment resulting from the1910 Mexican revolution. Owners of these mansions fled to the United States and Europe. I would person-ally hesitate to live in a place like this. They might put me away for delusions of grandeur. Rocendo and Carlene manage the place quite well with the help of Enrique who works for them. He made the fires for the cookout; he mixed the drinks, and helped in innumerable ways. Later in the evening he brought out his guitar and played and sang for us—music under the stars.

Un Bull

Take a tall glass and squeeze half a lime.

Add a jigger of rum, dark rum preferred.

Add half a teaspoon of simple syrup or dissolve half a teaspoon of sugar in the rum.

Fill glass with ice cubes.

Add a dash of Angostura bitters.

Fill glass with beer, dark beer preferred.

Garnish with wedge of lime and stir.

Es magnifico. Don't know why but some women are afraid of this drink. *Que triste.*

New Computer

Strange things have been happening with my computer. First thing to go was the spell checker. I think I wore it out. Then strange memory error warnings would appear on the monitor screen, and finally the system started to crash. These crashes were random occurrences but all too frequent. When I got a computer whiz to come out to the house, the computer would behave flawlessly. The last issue of **Letter from Mexico** was filled with so many errors I am terribly embarrassed and would like everyone to return these copies so that I can destroy them. I even misspelled Guanajuato.

Finally, I couldn't take it any longer and bought a new computer with lots of speed and a new set of programs. I'm a DOS and Word Perfect type of man, and although I can see that Microsoft Word can do a lot, how do you get the dang thing to do what you want it to do. I hired a young woman who teaches the Spanish version of Word to government workers, to come to the house and teach the programs to me in six lessons. The fact that she didn't speak English didn't bother me because you just push buttons and move the mouse around, right? Many computer terms in Spanish are the same in English. Like, *"Pleez cleeek de mouse,"* or, *"Pleez deleeet"* After three lessons, I told her this wasn't working out; let me struggle with this next addition of the newsletter and I would get back to her with a bunch of questions. First on my list is how to get rid of the Wizard Program Assistant. For those of you not familiar with the Wizard, the one on my computer looks like Einstein and makes mindless clicking noises. That little S.O.B. keeps running out in front of my page blocking what I want to do next. I find this guy so irritating that I think they should force Bill Gates to take him on as a roommate and spare the rest of us.

One thing that our new computer has brought us is the Internet. If you have any trouble reaching us by phone it's probably because I am on the Net. I know this must be old hat to many of you, but I can't get over the enormous array of information that this makes possible. I am fascinated by the history of Mexico and Mexican-American relations and have started making some searches. For example, I was interested in learning about the peace treaty, the Treaty of Guadalupe Hidalgo, which settled the war between Mexico and the US. I learned that our special negotiator, William Trist, disregarded a recall to Washington and negotiated the treaty in violation of most of his instructions. Moreover, when the US Senate took up the ratification of the treaty it unilaterally struck out Article XX of the treaty. This article provide some assurances of the property rights of Mexicans living in the ceded territory of over half of Mexico.

I learned about Marshall Bernardo Galvez, Governor of Spanish Louisiana, an area that extended from Texas to Florida and up to Georgia. Using troops from Mexico, Cuba, Haiti, Venezuela, and what is now the Dominican Republic he defeated the British in Baton Rouge, Mobile, Pensacola, and Fort Joseph Michigan—yes, Michigan. These victories relieved pressure on General Washington. It is claimed that there were more Hispanics fighting against the British than there were troops under the command of Washington. They named Galveston, Texas after Galvez. As a little Mexican-American boy I think I must have been sick and missed the day in school when they taught this in my American History class. At any rate it's fascinating stuff.

12

September 1998

Is Mexico Safe for Americans? Quality, Travels in Mexico, Cuernavaca, Oaxaca

Is Mexico Safe for Americans?

Occasionally our friends send us newspaper clippings about how dangerous it is to visit Mexico. If you follow American news reports, Mexico comes off as a violent country, not safe like the United States. Now from our perspective, we are always shocked to read the United States papers outlining narco-trafficking, kidnapping, murdering, robbing, mother raping, baby raping, prom girls killing their babies, parents killing their little girls, kids shooting their parents, teachers, and classmates, survivalists shooting it out with law enforcement agents, nannies choking the babies they are caring for. Such a list of actual events in the U.S. appears to be the worst of Court TV. But, just for a moment, imagine that you were living outside of the U.S. and that you assumed that all the violence that is taking place in the U.S. is somehow occurring in proximity to your loved ones outside the country. You probably would hope that they would move out as quickly as they could. America is a big country and violence is spread out over the land, with certain areas (areas that we tend to avoid) having a larger share of crime than our own neighborhoods. I believe it is the same here, and the question of whether Mexico is safe for Americans has about as much meaning as asking if Mexico is safe for bulls. The answer depends on whether the bull is in the *Plaza de Toros* or on a stud farm. In my case, well, I'm at neither. Although I do have concern for our security, in all honesty I feel as safe here as I did in Madison, Wisconsin, which has a pretty low crime rate. In a May 27 article the *Los Angeles Times* reported: "Most of the Mexican destinations frequented by American tourists—resorts such as Cabo San Lucas, Cancun, Puerto Vallarta, and also colonial cities like Guanajuato, San Miguel de Allende and Morelia—continue to do business as usual, with no reports of unusual threats to visitors."

On the whole, authorities say, resort areas have suffered relatively little in Mexico's run of troubles. "I can not recall us ever having any particular problems with Mexican ports of call," says Carnival Cruise line spokesperson, Jennifer De La Cruz." (How's that, for the name of a cruise line spokesperson?) "In all, the line has seven ships calling weekly at Mexican ports."

John Slocum, President of Amerispan Unlimited, a Philadelphia company that arranges Latin American language study trips for Americans, says he has been receiving more phone calls from concerned customers in the aftermath of recent television newsmagazine reports about crime in Mexico. But Slocum says that he's seen no change in reports on the experiences of Americans he has directed to Mexico. "In the last six months", Slocum said, "his company has sent roughly 200 students to Mexican language schools, and in that time, the worst crime his customers have reported is the disappearance of $20 from a guest's room night stand".

While Carole and I feel personally secure in Guanajuato, what about security for our property? This is a little bit different. Someone once mentioned to me that in Manhattan, a "BMW" emblem on an automobile translates to "Break My Window!" Having a luxury car like a BMW is practically an invitation for someone to break in. Here in Guanajuato, an unlocked house, or one that looks like it would be easy to enter, is virtually an invitation for burglars, usually young men. For example, our house was burgled before our front wall was completed. I'm not sure how the burglar got in, but here are some of the circumstances surrounding the crime.

Carole and I had gone to a movie at about five o'clock. The neighborhood night watchman does not come on duty until seven, which is an hour or so after the workmen building houses on our street leave for the day. There is a telephone pole next to the wall in front of our place that has those iron rod steps that the phone company installs for the convenience of their linemen. Apparently, I left a sliding glass door unlocked because it was wide open when we returned and the glass wasn't broken. The night watchman, who was guarding the construction next door, met the burglar and spoke with him. The burglar said he was looking for us and claimed I was his uncle. Domingo, the night watchman, who, I hate to say, has never struck me as being the brightest lantern on the block, told him we had gone to a movie and wouldn't be back for a few hours. The burglar replied that this was O.K.; he would wait. Later, he entered our house and took our Fax machine, a camera, a bunch of compact disks (Mexican music only), a few other things, and a bag to carry it all in. We have subsequently corrected a number of shortcomings in our home security. I took the iron steps off the telephone pole, we had the wall built to a greater height, we planted a type of bougainvillea that has thorny spines along the front wall, we now have a routine for locking the various sliding glass doors, and we supplemented Domingo's salary so that he would be on the lookout for us as well as the building project he was already guarding. In other words, we don't want our place to be the "BMW" of houses.

Another way of measuring the safety of our property is to look at the cost of our home insurance. Mexican insurance companies are not very competitive, but we were pleasantly surprised that the cost of our policy, which includes fire, floods, winds, earthquakes, and *burglaries,* is only $123 per year. If burglaries were all that frequent, wouldn't one expect to pay a whole lot more than $123? There is one catch, and that is the burglary must have resulted from a forced entry. This gets us back to the importance of carefully locking up.

But what about the basic honesty of the people in Guanajuato? Let me relate three incidents. At our first Christmas in Guanajuato we were getting ready for one of Dolores Riley's great Christmas dinners. She does the heavy-duty cooking, and the rest of us bring a dish to pass. Carole had me go to the market to get some garnish for her platter. The market was packed with people getting things for Christmas. I went to various stalls and purchased the items on my list. When I left the market, I discovered that I didn't have my wallet. My immediate reaction was to think that my pockets had been picked. That's what I had heard happened to Americans in Mexico City, so, naturally, I assumed it was what had just happened to me in Guanajuato. Without much hope of retrieving my billfold, I nevertheless retraced my steps, asking the various owners of the stalls I had visited if they had seen a wallet. Each shopkeeper stopped selling his wares and asked people to stand back so that he could check the place over. Finally, I arrived at one of the produce stands where the young owner immediately reached over to a shelf in back of him and pulled out my wallet with everything intact. He refused any kind of reward.

It happened again a couple of years later during the annual Cervantino Festival when thousands of people come to Guanajuato. I was getting out of a cab and unbeknownst to me my wallet stuffed with all my credit cards, photocopies of my passport and FM-3 permit and some money fell out of my pocket and landed on the curb. When I discovered it missing, I reported the loss to the police with little hope of finding my wallet. About three days later I received a call from a staff person at the University of Guanajuato who said he had found my wallet. The money was gone, but everything else was there.

And just the other day at the fish market, I left my wallet on the counter. (I'm going to have to get one of those chains that deliverymen use to attach their wallets to their pants.) The shop girl called me on the phone to tell me she had it. Would I have fared as well in Madison? I like to think so, but I'm really not sure. What do you think?

Quality

She was standing at the bus stop in front of the entrance to the Feranti-Packard Transformer plant. Attractive, neatly dressed, and holding a new brief case, the young woman was waiting for the bus. I had just dropped Derek Young off at the plant gate. His car was in the repair garage, and I didn't mind the drive of a few miles into the Mexican countryside where the plant is located. I stopped to ask her if she wanted a ride to *El Centro* where I was going. She gladly accepted as the next bus from the Village of Santa Teresa headed for Guanajuato would probably require a long wait.

Although she was dressed up in female executive garb, I didn't really believe that one so young could work at the plant. I asked her anyway if she was employed there. Feranti-Packard, a subsidiary of Rolls Royce of England, makes electric transformers, the big ones you see at electric substations. The young woman gave me a yes and no type of answer to my question, but after a lot of explaining in two languages, I learned that she was interning at the plant. "In what?" I asked, and she told me in "quality control." She was studying to be a quality control engineer at the University of Guanajuato.

Now during my occasional uncharitable moments, the very notion of quality control in this country conjures up—har, har, har—Mexican efficiency expert, honest government official, on-time appointments, and other slams, some deserved and some not. Somehow, it is hard to overcome ones preconceptions about Mexico's ability to produce quality products making the concept of the need for quality control engineers somewhat moot. What I have learned from Derek, however, is that quality is very high at this Feranti-Packard plant and that the Mexican workers here in Guanajuato were the equal to, or superior of, similar workers both in Canada as well as England.

A few miles down the road from Feranti-Packard is the big sprawling General Motors of Mexico assembly plant. They make light trucks, Suburbans, and sports utility vehicles. This new assembly plant was relocated from Mexico City in an effort to decentralize industry and employment and reduce congestion and pollution in the Federal District. The new plant is said to have GM's highest rating for quality production. I read recently in Newsweek magazine that some of the *maq-uiladora* plants that are manufacturing electronic goods along the border are producing products of exceptional quality. Some of these factories are starting to engage in more challenging manufacturing tasks instead of mindless assembly work.

What we are more accustomed to in Mexico are hand-made crafts. There is an old Mexican saying that if an article made by the hand of man were perfect, that this would be an affront to God, God being the only one who can make something perfect. In our house, we have various Mexican handcrafted articles including some hand blown glasses, each one a little different in height, diameter, and color. This variance is the charm of these items but we wouldn't want our TV screen to be lopsided. It's my hope that Mexico can retain its artisanal heritage while developing a tradition of quality. I think they can do this, particularly if they train enough pretty girls in quality control.

Travels in Mexico

Cuernavaca

Last summer we were invited by our friends, Gus and Marina Garcia and Juan and Marta Cotera, of Austin, Texas to join them in a trip to Oaxaca in July of this year to attend the *Guelaguetza,* the famous Oaxaca corn festival. At first I was a little reluctant to get involved in a Mexican version of a corn festival. Having lived in Madison, Wisconsin which is just a few miles from Sun Prairie, home of the famous Sun Prairie Corn Festival, I felt that I had already experienced the ultimate in corn fests. If I remember correctly, the Sun Prairie version starts out with the selection of a Corn Princess. No mere beauty contest this, the Princess's coronet goes to the young lady who sells the most tickets, thus exemplifying midwestern practicality for avoiding budget deficits for events of this kind, while rewarding initiative and enterprise. The main feature of the festival is that you can eat—for free—all the corn you want. The corn is carried into the festival grounds by large forklift trucks carrying vats of steaming sweet corn from the local cannery. Nothing else stands out about the event except that our son Nate won a goldfish in a ring toss game.

With this background in corn festivals, I was inclined to pass up the Oaxaca event except that the Garcias and the Coteras are such an interesting and fun group to be with that we didn't want to miss it. The first leg of the trip took us to

Cuernavaca. Once we got off the superhighway the road wound around through some picture-postcard scenery. We had heard so many horror tales about Mexico City that we wanted to plan our trip to Oaxaca to avoid the Capital. This was a bit tricky because all roads lead to Mexico City, but by circling around we reached Cuernavaca without entering the "Big M." We had never been to Cuernavaca, but it sounded like an interesting place. It is said that the rich and powerful from Mexico City have been drawn to the town since Cortez. They call it the land of perpetual spring.

We had a fine meal at an attractive restaurant, **La India Bonita,** which at one time was the home of Dwight Morrow, U.S. Ambassador to Mexico in the 1920's. Charles Lindbergh, while on a tour of Mexico after his famous flight, met his future wife, Anne Morrow at this home where they fell in love. The gardens are lovely and one can imagine America's "Lone Eagle" ending his loneliness in this setting. The name of the restaurant refers to the wife of the Emperor Maximillian's gardener. Maximillian fell in love with her and built a house that the Mexican's call the "House of Forgetfulness". The place he built had a suite of rooms for *La India Bonita*, but somehow he forgot to build a bedroom for his wife, the Empress. (Probably, one of those short-term memory lapses.)

While in Cuernavaca we visited the Cathedral *de la Asuncion*. Begun under Cortez in 1526, this fortress-like church revealed an unexpected thing to us: renovators in the 1960's exposed Japanese-style paintings depicting the persecution of Christians in Japan. The murals are huge and cover both main walls. In the front of the church is a skull and crossbones carved in stone above the entrance. I was unable to find out the story behind these depictions. Later, we visited the *Palacio de Cortez*. Cortez began this structure in 1522. The place is massive and cold. It is not difficult to imagine *El Conquistador* roaming the halls of his fortress castle pleased with his achievement in the conquest of Mexico. However, the massiveness of both of these buildings makes one wonder how secure the conquistadors felt about their triumph.

While staying in a small hotel in the colonial center of town, we chatted with some of the guests and asked how long it took to drive to Oaxaca, our next day's journey. One person said three hours, and another said it was three and one half. Four hours ought to cover it, I concluded, so we planned a noon departure. Once again much of the countryside was spectacularly beautiful as we traveled the well-paved, two-lane, winding road through the mountains to Oaxaca. The truth is it is a seven-hour journey. Carole has an absolute policy that we don't drive at night in Mexico. I have an absolute policy that we don't sleep in fields at night in Mexico. As the sky started to fade we finally reached the superhighway toll road for the last forty miles to our destination.

Oaxaca

We came loaded with all sorts of information about Oaxaca including, of course, the name of the hotel where Marta Cotera had made reservations for all of us. *Las Golandrinas* was to be our home for the next few days. The colonial center of Oaxaca was teeming with people and traffic was unreal. We stopped to ask some policemen where Hotel *Las Golandrinas* was located. They said they had never heard of it. "What was the address," they asked. We didn't have an address, just a name. Finally, I double parked in front of a government building that had some people standing outside and inquired if they knew where our hotel was. Someone went inside and returned with the information. Just as I was trying to absorb the directions a huge intercity bus, no longer willing to wait for us, blasted its horn for us to stop blocking the street. We circled several blocks so that we could return and get the rest of the directions.

Las Golandrinas turned out to be a little jewel of a hotel, and just $26 a night. The rooms were small and simple but immaculately clean. They were arranged around three small patios beautifully landscaped with flowers, fruit trees, and potted plants. The pots were encrusted with flowers and animals in relief of a type not common in Guanajuato. It made me want a garden like this in Guanajuato. I had thought our garden was coming along nicely, but after seeing the garden's lushness at *Las Golandrinas*, it seemed to me what we had was dull. We sat out on these patios shooting the breeze with fellow guests or just swinging in the hammock and watching the humming birds do their thing.

What we didn't know is that Juan Cotera is a very good friend of Martine Ruiz Camino, director of Oaxaca's State Tourism Office. Apparently, Juan had called Señor Camino's office for assistance in our obtaining a hotel reservation. Word must have filtered down, because the Coteras, Garcias and their in-laws, the Lopezes, were greeted at the airport by a young woman, Marie Carmen, PhD. Señorita Carmen's doctorate is in history, and she spent the next several days with us as our full-time guide, the best way to be introduced to a new city. We were driven to an auditorium connected with the State Office of Tourism for a banquet honoring the dancers of the *Guelaguetza*. The *Guelaguetza* is a marvelous tradition dating back to the fifteenth century, derived from the pre-Columbian celebration of rites dedicated to the adoration and petitioning of the Aztec goddess "Centeotl," patroness of corn. In her honor they performed dances and ritual feasts which culminated in the sacrifice of a virgin who, during the festivities, was regarded as the incarnation of the goddess herself. For the updated version of the *Guelaguetza* (no sacrifice), there must have been 700 performers and guests. I was surprised that Carole and I were included among the small group of people introduced at the banquet. Also introduced was Centeotl herself. Not a corn princess, not a corn queen, not a beauty queen, she was a **goddess**. With her gracious smile and sparkling eyes, she had a remarkable presence as she stepped to the microphone to give a speech, first in Mixtec and then in Spanish. How could this four foot six, eighteen-year-old woman, dressed in a *huipile,* the square cut beautifully adorned shirt-like dress of her pueblo, cast such an enchanting spell? Awe came over the audience. The panel that had selected her included anthropologists and historians who granted her this honor due to her knowledge of her people and her ability to speak in her native language as well as in Spanish. We were told that her two speeches were extemporaneous. They sounded flawless to me, and the Mixtec sounded like poetry. We later learned that she would be starting pre-med studies at the University in the fall.

Dancers from different parts of the State of Oaxaca along with half dozen bands were in the auditorium and performed a preview of the forthcoming *Guelaguetza*. The male dancers, always dressed in muslin, were excellent dancers, but the women stole the show with their stunning variety of costumes. When you see a travel poster of Mexico that includes women dressed in native costume, it is most likely to be women from Oaxaca. Some were dressed with coils of black wool on their heads that made them look like Japanese geisha. Many others had a unique headdress made by wrapping a *reboso* (long shawl or scarf) into an interesting knot. I asked Marie Carmen if she knew how to tie one of these knots and she shook her head no.

One group of about twenty-five dancers dressed in highly decorated *huipiles* and the intricate headdress I just mentioned came onto the floor first holding pineapples on their shoulders and then over their heads. They waved them to and fro in a beguiling fashion all the while smiling demurely as they danced. Later they put down their pineapples and formed a single close line, arms joined to each other's waists, and danced barefoot in unison across the floor to music that grew ever louder. Marie Carmen said they had been tagged "The Indian Rockettes." The most beautiful costumes of all were the ones worn by the women of the Isthmus of Tehuantapec. Known for their grace, wit, charm and haughty deportment and poise when walking, their costume is internationally famous. They wear a white accordion-pleated head tunic extending about fourteen inches completely around their head. Small flowers are embroidered on their dresses and they are festooned in gold jewelry, which stands out with their elaborate costume and dark skin. There are several stories that explain the unique pleated headdress. It gets very hot where these women come from and in the early days when the Spanish first arrived the women went bare-chested. One version is that a ship ran aground near their pueblo and a trunk-full of petticoats washed ashore. The women didn't know what to do with them so they made headdresses out of them. Another version is that the Dominican Friars were alarmed at their attire, or lack thereof, and gave them a tunic to cover their chests. This was a wimple that covered the head and hung down over the wearer's back and front with a white border cloth around the face. Apparently they turned this "garment" upside down to form a headdress leaving their breasts exposed. Must have looked stunning. The blouses they now wear were a later addition.

Another group of young women dancers from Oaxaca's coastal area danced in what I can only describe as a spunky style. They would interrupt their dance every once in a while for one of the dancers to make some bawdy remarks in Spanish. The guidebook describes it as "Humorous and sometimes offensive verses are recited in mountain Zapotec." I could understand only one of the young women dancers who said something in Spanish like: "I'm a jalapeno pepper and I'm plenty hot. Why don't you take a <u>bite</u> out of me?" It sounded better in Spanish, but you get the idea. One of my favorite groups, even livelier than the previous, was a group of young men and women dancers who swirled gaily around the stage. The women play the part of the bull and they do their best to knock the men over by butting them with their heads. It's hilarious to see the women, pigtails flying, butting the men and even as the men start to get up, butting them again and again. They seemed to enjoy doing this even as much as we enjoyed watching it. At the conclusion of each delegation's dance, the dancers threw products from their hometowns into the audience: baked goods, oranges, small bottles of Mescal, even pineapples and coconuts. Fortunately, we were outside firing range and weren't in risk of getting beened on the head with a coconut or bottle of Mescal. This was great fun for the crowd and is part of an old tradition of each group sharing what it has with its neighbors. Oaxaca revels and celebrates its diversity—ethnic, cultural and physical. Sixteen distinct ethnic groups live here with as many different languages. There is an interplay of two trends: diversity among culturally and linguistically distinct groups and unity through interaction and communication among the groups. How marvelous it is to encounter this as a living fact rather than merely a goal.

At one evening event we were given seats directly behind a delegation of ambassadors to Mexico and their wives. I didn't see our new U.S. Ambassador to

Mexico and wondered why he wasn't on the job. And speaking of important personages, President Zedillo was in Oaxaca when we first arrived. He was there to dedicate the restoration of the former convent of *Santo Domingo*. This is the grandest and costliest restoration in Latin America and is one of the largest cultural centers on the continent. We have an American friend, June Jackson, who lives in Guanajuato. June once remarked of her visit to Oaxaca: "I'm a Protestant, but if I were ever to convert to Catholicism, my visit to the church of *Santo Domingo* would be what would do it." We visited this magnificent church and convent during Sunday mass. This is the most beautiful church I have ever seen, and believe me, I have seen the Frank Lloyd Wright-designed Unitarian church in Madison. It doesn't compare.

The following Monday, the same dances were performed at the actual *Guelaguetza,* only in longer and more complete versions. The event was held in a special stadium built for this program and located where it is said the Indians held their *Guelaguetza* prior to the Spanish conquest. One could see the colonial center of the city directly in back of the stadium. Our seats were high up and in back of the stand of the *Guelaguetza* officials and The Goddess Centeotl. In our elite section, straw hats were handed out to people who were bare headed. Cool bottled water was dispensed along with a refreshing rice drink with pieces of fruit. That afternoon we were taken to a country restaurant with about nine hundred other people. We were greeted at the entrance by several young señoritas who passed out six-inch lengths of bamboo that were filled with mescal by other beautiful young women. Mescal is similar to tequila. One of the differences in the drinks is that mescal has a *gusano* worm in the bottom of the bottle, proof that you have the real thing. Further into the restaurant, we saw two women frothing up a batch of *pulque,* a fermented low-alcohol beverage that I have tried but have failed to acquire a taste for. (Pulque is even given to pregnant women for health reasons. Some very elegant people, as well as common folk, say they like it, but I can tell you it's really pretty bad stuff.) What beer is to Milwaukee, mescal is to Oaxaca. Bottles of a house brand mescal were on all the tables. I was much taken by the label which read: *Restaurant Tipico "La Capilla" Frente a la Gasolinera, Zaachila. Oax.* Pretty classy booze, this "front of the gasoline station" stuff. The food kept coming all afternoon. It was delicious, but they might consider changing the name of the restaurant to *El Colesterol.*

Our driver and Marie Carmen took us to El Tule, which has an enormous tree alleged to be 2000 years old. Its trunk is forty-eight feet in circumference. We were shown a *tourist yu u,* a guesthouse built in the artisan villages of the Valley of Oaxaca. Visitors are permitted to live in the village and observe or learn native weaving or some other craft. These attractive and well-constructed dormitories are turned over to the villages that maintain them and derive any revenues. This was a new project initiated by Martinez Ruiz Camino to bring some economic activity to the pueblos.

In one of the towns we visited, there was a *quincianera* procession headed for the church. This is a ceremony for girls when they turn fifteen. A mariachi band of the highest caliber headed the procession. They played sweet music and all instruments were in tune. The celebrated young woman was resplendent in a long dress with heavy gold brocade. They marched into the church and we followed. A few minutes later, a second *quincianera* procession came up the street. The girl was no less pretty although she was less elaborately adorned. She was preceded by the village brass band. The party stopped under one of the huge shade trees in front of the church and waited their turn for the church. One of the girl's uncles explained that today was devoted to the serious part of the "coming out", but tomorrow they would have a big fiesta. In the next village we encountered another procession en route to their church preceded by that village's brass band. This procession was a wedding, the bride in a long white gown and the groom a young military officer in white dress tunic and lots of gold braid. I complimented Marie Carmen and her department for arranging so many colorful processions for us.

We visited two archeological sites: Mitla and Monte Alban. Of the two sites Monte Alban is the most awesome. It is like nothing I have ever seen and I can't begin to do it justice. I do recall a couple of years ago when Carole and I were visiting Patzquaro to buy carved doors for our house, that we ran into a chemistry teacher who taught in a California college that had a lot of minority students. He said he and his wife traveled to Mexico every summer, and one year they took along one of his students, a young Chicano. When they visited Monte Alban the boy was speechless and finally said with great amazement, "They never told us about this!"

The layout of the city of Oaxaca follows classic Spanish colonial town planning practice—large rectangular blocks, a central plaza, or *zocolo*, with cathedral and government palace on two sides, and arcades with businesses on the opposite sides. One evening we went to the *zocolo* for a drink and a bite to eat. The *zocolo* was filled with vendors with mariachis and a marimba band playing for diners at the outdoor arcade restaurants. Just as we started to head for our hotel it started to rain. All taxis were occupied so we set forth on foot with me in the lead. I heard a few faint protests over the direction I was pursuing, but I was very sure that I knew the way—four blocks to the left and six blocks to the right—my parade followed. After having completed the four-block and six-block trek, maps started to come out and there was talk of mutiny even though the rain was light. Fortunately for us, two women drove by and seeing us standing in the rain examining maps, stopped to give us help. They claimed we had gone in the opposite direction and were, literally, off the map. We then reversed our direction, now traveling twelve blocks in one direction and eight blocks in another. I still can't figure out how the whole city of Oaxaca revolved 180 degrees that night with the *zocolo* being the pivot point.

Carole and I were left to our own devices for a day and stopped at a patio coffeehouse. While enjoying some of Oaxaca's famous hot chocolate, an old Indian woman came over to us carrying a basket. She reached into the basket and pulled out a pinch-full of a very dark reddish substance that looked like it may have been shredded. She ate it and said, "Try it, it's good". "No thanks," I protested. "Just try it," she said forcefully as she chomped it down, "it's *chapulin.*" So I tasted it. I couldn't place the flavor. It was good in a strange way but completely different from anything I had experienced. It tasted slightly of dried shrimp. As we examined it closely, we could make out that it was tiny, tiny grasshoppers that had been dried or fried. We later learned that there is an old saying in Oaxaca: once you have eaten *chapulin,* you will return in the future. I'm sure we will, hopefully soon and many times, but I think that my eating grasshoppers one time should hold us for all future return visits.

13

November 1998

Quiz, Illegal Immigration, Trip to Rio de Bravo, Tit for Tat, Fifty Years Ago, La Gruta, Christmas Greetings

Quiz

What does Mexico have seven of, Italy have thirteen of, Spain have ten of, France have five of, the United Kingdom have two of, and the United States have one of? Give up? The answer is World Heritage Cities. This is a designation by UNESCO of cities of such beauty and historic value that they should remain part of the world's patrimony, cities that belong to all of us. These are a group of one hundred and fifty one cities that should be lovingly cared for and preserved. They are not reconstructions like Williamsburg, but living cities that have come down to us in tact through time.

Guanajuato is one of seven cities in Mexico that claim this distinction, along with Queretaro, Mexico City, Morelia, Oaxaca, Puebla, and Zacatecas. I have frequently written in **Letter from Mexico** of the beauty and charm of this town we live in. In truth, the place affects people in different ways. For example, one visitor who came here a few years ago looked out from one of the *miradors*, scenic outlooks, on the panoramic highway that circumferentially traverses Guanajuato and exclaimed: "It sure makes you appreciate what you have at home." Here is this visitor to this city with its churches, ex-haciendas, aqueducts, its narrow cobblestone streets, its subterranean roadways, its historic buildings, and colorful houses hanging on the hillside and yes a lot of poor people's houses too and what did she see, well she saw the poor peoples houses and she saw the roadside litter. This is part of Guanajuato for sure, but to a lot of us this is an enchanting city. Another visitor to our place, James Smith from Austin Texas, on driving through the *subteraneo*, that partly underground vehicular passage way that weaves its way through the center of Guanajuato, remarked that Guanajuato would be a great site for filming a Dracula movie. Well, in spots it is a little gothic in appearance.

This wouldn't be much of a quiz if it only had had one question so here goes Question Number 2. What is the only city in the United States of America that qualified for designation as a World Heritage City? This is a toughy and if you get this right go to the front of the geography class. Hint: Ocir Otreup Nauj Nas. Please write to me if you didn't get it and I will send you more hints.

According to what I have learned about World Heritage Cities on the internet, a few years ago, Japan which has two cities designated, Kyoto and Kamitaira, wanted to add Hiroshima as a third site. They sought inclusion because of its being the site of the dropping of the first atom bomb. The United States and the Peoples Republic of China vehemently opposed inclusion of Hiroshima as not meeting the criteria for a World Heritage City and won out, thus demonstrating what can be accomplished through Sino-American cooperative effort.

Illegal Immigration

It was about 1960 when I was county planning in Manitowoc Wisconsin that Harlan Schwartz and I drove to Milwaukee to hear Buckminster Fuller give a lecture on the history of architecture at Downer College. Fuller, you might recall, was the inventor of the geodesic dome, the dymaxium house, the principal of tensegrity as he termed it, which made possible the building of enormous light weight space frames using the tensile strength of steel wire pitted against the compressive strength of light aluminum rods, and much more. He coined the term spaceship earth and that was a long time ago.

I still remember quite distinctly some of the things Fuller had to say that evening. His lecture went on for two hours. Fuller started out by telling us that on the east coast of Africa along the 1000-mile coastline of the Sultanate of Oman, wooden boats of a distinctive design called dhows have been used for 4000 years to ply the Indian Ocean. The sailors that manned these dhows transported herbs and spices from Iran and Yemen, gold and colored fabrics from India and timber from east Africa. The dhows were very well designed, excellently made and are still in use today much as they were in the past.

Buckminster Fuller said that when this part of east Africa was under the control of the British the colonial authorities had a continuing problem with smuggling by the dhow seamen. They sent various authorities to look into the problem but it was not until they sent a certain perspicacious administrator to study the problem that they got a handle on it. This man, Lord something or other, sat down with the Arab chieftains on the sandy shores of the sea and listened to what the Arabs had to say. Fuller explained that the Arabs had always excelled in mathematics and so it was very soon that the chieftain took a twig and traced on the sand a Cartesian graph with time tracked horizontally along the base and quantity of dhow trading along the vertical, not to be confused with Dow-Jones trading. The wise old chief traced a line that kept rising with the passage of time and explained that this trading had been going on for centuries. The British Empire, he went on, with all of its power and might, if it really made the effort could possibly reduce the increase in smuggling but could hardly stop or change this long-term upward trend. It would be best if you just accepted it.

Perhaps you are wondering as we did at the time we heard this lecture, what all this narrative had to do with architecture. Well I'm not quite sure I remember that part exactly but I think it had something to do with the building of boats. As Fuller explained, invert the hull of a boat and you have something that looks very much like the nave of a church. The word 'nave' comes from *navis* that means ship in Latin. And, perhaps you are wondering what all of this has to do with illegal immigration.

I would argue that the back and forth migration of illegal aliens from Mexico to the United States has been going on for decades perhaps for centuries. And that the United States with all its power and might, possibly could affect the long term trend a tad, but would really not be able to halt or significantly affect it. When the economy of Mexico goes down and unemployment of the poorest people in Mexico is up, out-migration increases. There are powerful forces at work here and unless the law of supply and demand is repealed not a whole lot can be done to stop it.

This is unacceptable to most Americans. As George Will on the question of illegal immigration once put it, every nation has the right to defend its borders. But just like Mexico had the right to defend its borders from the American Army of General Winnfield Scott in 1847 or the army of General John Pershing in the "Punitive Expedition" of 1916, Mexico wasn't successful. I don't suppose the Mexicans liked it but they finally came to accept it. I believe America needs to simply accept the idea of cross border migration as a fact of life.

But that doesn't mean that we can't deal constructively with the problem. At various times I have come upon someone here in Mexico who has been an illegal immigrant to the U.S. I suppose there must be some scoundrels among the people who dare to cross the border illegally but I must say that the several people I have met who mentioned that they had worked in the United States were really very fine people. Other Americans who live here have remarked the same thing as well. I guess when you actually get to know these people personally, one's attitude changes. The illegal migrants tend to be more energetic, they are incredibly hard working people—most of them do it for their families. Several with whom I spoke with were trying to save up enough so they could start a little business. Living here in Mexico where living can be so satisfying, one gets the feeling that these illegals, go to the U.S. not to cash in on welfare benefits or health care but for economic reasons. They are willing to take the lowest paid, nastiest jobs, without complaining. They do a lot of useful work for Americans. Of course, being illegal, they are easily exploited and mistreated by some of their employers as well as by some of their own people.

The benefit to the local economy is of enormous significance. One day while passing the local Western Union Office in the nearby town of Silao I noticed some women sitting on the curbstone in front of the office nursing their babies. They were waiting all day for the money wire to come in from the U.S. If the money sent by their husbands and sons were an aid program, I couldn't imagine a more efficient way of getting the money in the hands of those who need and deserve it more than with these transfers.

Why doesn't our government determine how many workers from Mexico we can use and arrange for them to come on a permit basis? This would be a more humane and satisfactory method as against having a bunch of illegals sneaking across the border. Is it possible that the real opposition to this comes from American employers that prefer the present arrangement in which they pay less than minimum wage? I don't know, but something appears amiss in the way the U.S. is dealing with this problem.

Last summer Carole and I traveled to San Antonio and Austin Texas to visit family and friends. Do you remember the pictures of a horrible drought in Texas and smoke filled skies from fires burning in Mexico and as far away as Guatemala. We drove through that and we noticed that Texas had more of an accumulation of smoke and dust than Mexico where most of it emanated. We saw a fleet of pick-up trucks loaded with policemen and soldiers gassing up to go fight the fires in the State of San Luis de Potosi. No fancy helicopters or cargo planes were present to fight the fires—just shovels. No doubt the exceptionally long dry summer had something to do with El Nino, but there has been a long-term trend of cutting trees faster than efforts to replant. Yes, there are conservation and environmental programs in Mexico but they are too little and too late. When we built our house we had to replace any trees we cut down on our lot. Today, this requirement has been expanded to even include the replacement of any cactus cut down with five new cactus plants. Enforcement is lax and so it's hard to see any real progress. So what does this have to do with illegal immigration, you ask?

Wouldn't it make sense for the United States to initiate a co-operative program with Mexico to hire young Mexican workers to improve the environment in Mexico? Not just as an aid program but a program in our own self-interest. Like illegal migration, pollution does not respect borders. Paying just a dollar an hour, thousands of young Mexicans would be receiving better than local minimum wage and making a substantial improvement in the environment of North America. Reforestation, stream bank improvement, wildlife habitat restoration, wastewater treatment system construction, landfill construction and much more could be undertaken. Employing this army of workers could also help reduce the pressure for migration to the U.S.

Trip to Rio de Bravo

As we have become more acquainted with Guanajuato, Carole and I have come across a couple of programs available to residents that we have found to be worthwhile. One of these comes from a government organization called ISSEN. Anyone living here who is sixty years or more in age is eligible. Carole didn't have any trouble qualifying but I just squeaked in. By receiving an ISSEN card one is entitled to discounts on all government sponsored cultural events and facilities such as the symphony concerts where we pay $2.50 instead of $5, movies where we pay, I think it is $1.40 instead of $2. It includes discounts on all bus, train and airfares within the Republic and museum entrance fees.

Another organization we have joined is Friends of the Alhondiga de Granaditus Museum, discussed in Chapter 9, *Museums of Guanajuato*. The Friends are a group of what appears to be mainly retired Mexicans. They raise money for the museum mainly through dues and arranging some low cost trips for its members to various points of interest in Mexico. We have not been able to partake in many of these trips but we did go on one trip to Valle del Bravo, which is a town and artificial lake in the State of Mexico west of Mexico City. This is a place where several former presidents of Mexico and a number of wealthy and super wealthy Mexicans have vacation homes. We had never heard of Valle del Bravo. Some people suggested that the place was kind of a little secret the Mexicans had. I rather doubt that because it is featured on a Mexican postage stamp used for letters to the United States.

The trip consisted of two nights, with meals for three days plus bus transportation all for $150 per person. The route took us through small towns and scenic countryside. One of the small towns we stopped at had an enormous gold and silver mine that was attempting a comeback after a disastrous fire of many years ago In the town square was a long wall with a quotation carved in stone from a woman that had owned the mine. Apparently, her oldest son was kidnapped and held for ransom, during some revolutionary times. The abductors wanted her to turn over the mine to them. The lady's famous quotation: "Better that you take all my children than I accede to your outrageous demands." That's pretty tough, Mom. No way would I ever want to cross this woman.

The town of Valle del Bravo is loaded with shops where the local Indians sell their handicraft wares. I had noticed that in Guanajuato the indigenous women never, never, wore double braids. I had wondered if they thought that made them look too Indian. Around our town it seems that they all wear a gingham apron in one of two colors, red or brown, over a plane dress and they have a fulsome single braid of very black hair. In Valle del Bravo the Indian women wore red skirts and white embroidered blouses and double braids with very black hair. At any rate they were colorful and quite striking. Our tour included a boat trip on the large lake. Vacation mansions lined certain sections of the lake shoreline. The sky was filled with hang-gliders, and parasails. In the evening we saw glowing balls of fire sail over the lake. These were referred to as *globos*. This was a nostalgic thing for me because I remember making the exact same type of hot air balloons with my brothers when we lived on Forest Park Boulevard in Janesville, Wisconsin. After Christmas we would collect tissue paper Christmas wrap from our house and our neighbors. The plan for these tissue paper balloons appeared in "A Boys Book of Mechanics,' which is out of print now but I think I could still duplicate the plans if anyone is interested. Tissue paper gores were cut out and pasted together to form a balloon in the shape of a light bulb about seven feet in height. A ball of twine connected to a cross wire frame attached to a circular ring, was dipped in kerosene and ignited to send it aloft. In Janesville, we launched these balloons during the day and watched them fly over the roofs of our neighbors' houses, praying that they would burn up in the air and spare the wooden shingled houses below. In Valle del Bravo, the balloons were launched at night. It was very beautiful to see these balls of fire glide over the city and the lake. Our traveling companions, Bob and Judith Patout, bought some of these *globos*. Well, actually it was Bob and I that bought them—I guess it's kind of a guy thing.

Our tour director announced that our itinerary for this trip included stops for an *aperitif* both on the way down as well as the return. The wayside that had been selected as a stop for this imbibing was closed so the director decided to pour the tequila and serve it to us on the bus as it moved along. Now most of the people on this bus were our age or older, a lot of them retired Mexican schoolteachers. The director pulled out a small boom box and played some tapes of Mexican music as we drank our tequila and listened to the singing and joking. Once you acquire a taste for it, tequila straight up is not at all a bad drink. Alcoholically, it is not as strong as bourbon, Scotch, or brandy, but capable of bringing out a lot of joy among a congenial group. It was great fun as we rocked our way back to Guanajuato.

Tit for Tat

I suppose it's only fare that the United States return the favor for all the drugs that pass through Mexico and end up in the U.S. I'm speaking of the cigarettes sold here by American tobacco companies. Facing enormous pressure to reduce the number of underage smokers in the U.S., the beleaguered American cigarette manufacturers have been retiring Joe Camel and the Marlboro Man. Not retired exactly, it's more like they have been given Foreign Service jobs so that these companies can remain profitable.

Smoking is popular here and as far as I can see, it isn't restrained in any way in restaurants and public places except by an individual's notion of courtesy. I have noticed on several occasions that often two men will meet and one will offer a cigarette to the other, who thereupon places the cigarette in a pocket to savor it later. I notice that a lot of young women, it almost seems more than men, smoking on the street and in cafes. Fortunately, many of the restaurants we favor are outdoors. One day I saw two attractive young blond women with two equally attractive young men climb into a mint condition Oldsmobile convertible, perhaps 1960 vintage, and drive slowly down the street giving away Marlboro cigarettes not to the likes of me, but to young folks. The young people in the car were dressed in white letter sweaters and I tried to remember where I had seen kids like this before. It took me awhile but I finally came to me. It was a homecoming parade where the Battling Bluebirds of Janesville High School met the Madison East High School Purgolders. It's amazing that a cigarette company could so faithfully re-enact a scene like that. Thank you Mr. Marlboro Man.

Fifty Years Ago

Shortly after the end of World War II one of our neighbors in Janesville, Don Peacock and his young wife, moved to Mexico to study under the GI Bill. Don has been receiving **Letter from Mexico** and he has told me that he enjoyed reading them. I recently asked him if he would describe some of his experiences back then. He has kindly accepted and sent this delightful and vivid recollection, which I think you will enjoy.

Entonses y Pues

Exactly fifty years ago, from 1947-48, I was a graduate student at Mexico City College. Leaving the University of Wisconsin, Madison as newlyweds, we were eager to experience new cultures, adventures, and especially travel opportunities.

We lived in a rented gatehouse of an *hacienda*-cum-poultry farm, elevated and overlooking the Valley of Mexico, near the quaint suburb of San Angel. Our magnificent view to the east encompassed the snowcapped twin peaks of Popocateptl and Ixtaccihuatl. Our rent was $35 a month, furnished one bedroom, one bath, a fireplace in the corner of the living room, and a unique kitchen with only three walls; the open side was a huge pepper tree, anchoring a flagstone patio-terrace. Neighborhood expatriates mostly Germans, came to our door to protest the $1 per day wage we paid our Indian maid, saying You God damn Americans are ruining our good deal here!" We bought Elena, the maid, a tabletop washing machine that she refused to use, preferring to pound (and ruin) my dress shirts on a flat rock on a creek-side laundry. The maids loved to gather there and exchange gossip about their crazy gringo employers.

Personal hygiene was a challenge as we used a *rapido* water heater, fired by wooden sticks to generate maybe twenty gallons of tepid shower water. We were allocated a quick and brisk three minutes to shower two or three times a week as the maid kept loading more wood into the *rapido* firebox. The French say we are too obsessed with frequent bathing anyway!

As the college was twenty miles away, for transport we purchased a yellow 1938 Sunbeam Talbot convertible. The seller was Pepe de Parada, an elegant aristocrat. Then agent/manager for Guest Airlines; Pepe is ninety-something years old now and still has "an eye" for the ladies, or so his niece who was visiting in Vail tells us. He bought the car, known to local police as *El Limonocito*, from Rita Guggenheim who had smuggled it into Veracruz from Havana in the pre-Castro years. The car was never properly registered so, lacking all the important official documents could not be taken out of Mexico. I still cry when recalling a forced sale of the car for $750—one of life's bigger mistakes, but I digress.

To keep things in proper perspective regarding dirt-cheap housing, cars, beer, tacos, our income then was a paltry $105 a month from the GI Bill and several cash wedding presents. Unmarried veteran/students received a stipend of $75 a month—at that time mucho pesos! I recall the following bureaucratic snafu—Mel Franks from Los Angeles didn't receive his monthly $75 check for one year; repeated visits to our embassy finally disclosed that some idiotic clerk had been filing his checks in a pigeonhole under the name of Frank Mel! Mel Frank was borrowed out to the maximum around school.

One recalls little things like the peasant who brought burro loads of firewood to our door; the vegetable vendor who sold from his wheelbarrow two radishes, two eggs, two carrots, one onion, corn, etc. We had no refrigerator, only a small icebox, so one had to purchase necessities on a daily basis. I remember one vender who brought to the house small balls of unsalted butter, hand wrapped in dry cornhusks. Wonderful stuff! This fresh butter on equally fresh *bolios*, a hard crusted roll, was to die for.

Next doors to us was a small *ranchito*, housing the mistress of some Mexican Army colonel. Party noises wafting over our common wall made one wonder what in hell was going on over there. Orgies and drunkenness, I expect.

Fifty years ago, Mexico City had a population of two million, unlike the catastrophic megalopolis of over 20 million today. Then you could breath the clean air and see 80 to 100 miles across the valley—so unlike today's ecological disaster.

Thomas Wolfe said it best—you can't go back home. We returned to San Angel some years later to find our beautiful little gatehouse *casita* had been bulldozed down to make room for a superhighway. Gad, what a keen disappointment!

One final observation: We spent one Christmas holiday week in Acapulco, then a small resort before the Jet Set discovered its pleasures. Acapulco fifty years ago was utilized primarily by Mexicans on holiday from the Capitol, unlike the hordes of plastic waving tourists from Canada and the United States, together greatly diluting its charm. I chose to put all meals, hotel room charges, drinks and the like on a running tab and when I "settled up," the seven day holiday cost an amazing $75.U.S. That would buy you two decent dinners in Acapulco today.

The entire two years spent long ago in Mexico stand out now, especially as time winds down until those precious years, as the song goes, and we tend naturally as we look back on our lives. I am thankful for having had the opportunity to visit, observe, partake and savor the special wonders of Mexico and often wish I could return, but so like youth, it is impossible to reclaim once used. How sad that youth is wasted on the young.

La Gruta

Throughout Mexico and certainly in many parts of the State of Guanajuato, thermal waters abound, indicating an active geology. There is one place, Comanjila, which is about twenty miles west of Guanajuato which is a posh resort where you can "take the waters," have a mud bath, a steam bath, a massage, go swimming, eat drink, or stay overnight. For me there are too many Mercedes Benzes and snazzy cars in the parking lot for my wallet and I to feel comfortable. If getting in the water with these folks meant that some of their wealth would rub off on me, OK, I'll go for it. But I prefer simpler surroundings.

About twelve miles out of town on a road to nowhere is a little village called Cuevas that is said to have thermal baths. Carole and I drove out there one afternoon but it was getting late so we didn't have time to check out the baths. But recently, during a visit of our former neighbors in Madison, Wisconsin, Cliff and Colleen Germain, we tried out for the first time a Mexican thermal bath that is near San Miguel. San Miguel has several of these and we chose *La Gruta* that is about five miles north of town. The guidebook says they have three pools with thermal waters 112 degrees Fahrenheit. The waters are slightly astringent and have the same chemical composition as those in Baden Baden, Germany. It is said that they lessen the effect on aging.

I don't know if it took any years off of me, but I noticed Cliff Germain hopping around like a spring chicken once he stepped out of the grotto. Later when our daughter Jenny, came for a visit, we returned to *La Gruta* to soak. The water in pool number 1 is too cool for me, and the water in pool number 3 is too hot, but the water in pool number 2 is juuust right. This pool has seats made of cement at a level that keeps your torso under the water and your head out. A young waiter brings you a glass of excellent cold dark Mexican beer. I don't know how they do it in Baden Baden, but this was *bueno, bueno*.

Someone in Guanajuato mentioned that there is a couple that whenever they drive through Mexico they stop at <u>every</u> thermal spa they come across. I'd like to take that up too. It sounds like fun and not as strenuous as my other favorite activity, bungee jumping.

Christmas Greetings

Guanajuato, which I suspect is more of a traditionalist town than other cities in Mexico, seems to celebrate two kinds of Christmas. One has Santa Claus, American Christmas Carols, and Christmas trees. The trees are sold as *Arbol de Navidad*

Douglas. Somehow it just doesn't sound right to me. The big supermarket starts with this stuff just before Thanksgiving Day, although Thanksgiving is not a Mexican holiday. The other Christmas, the Mexican *Posada* is quite different. The *posadas* are *fiestas* preparing the way for the Mexican's biggest day of all, *La Navidad,* Christmas. *Posadas,* inns commemorate the journey of Mary and Joseph to Bethlehem. People join processions, chanting songs about their quest for a room. Afterward there are games, such as the breaking of *piñatas* filled with candy and fruit, which is broken by a blindfolded child wielding a stick. Here in Guanajuato many families put up a *naciamento*, a miniature clay replica of Bethlehem and the stable where Christ was born. Gifts are given, but only to the children, and on January 6 rather than Christmas day, because this is the day the Magi are suppose to have offered their presents to Jesus. At dinner on that day a large ring-like cake is served, inside which is hidden a figurine. The person who finds it has the honor of paying for the fiesta held on February 2, the *Candalaria* feast.

In our house we put up a small but well decorated artificial tree. Last year we but up a *naciamento*. We are not Catholic but didn't feel it would do any harm. The Mexicans here use moss on the floor of the miniature stable and so did we. It didn't work out because our cat Sara loved to tear up the moss and knock over the figurines.

We want to send Holiday greetings to all our friends in the U.S. and here in Mexico. Have a very merry Christmas, happy Hanukah, and a great New Year.

Love,

Charlie and Carole Montemayor

14

February 1999

Battle of Santa Rosa, Trip to the Pacific Beaches

Battle of Santa Rosa

All day long the battle raged. The first skirmish started when the Spanish fusiliers advanced down the main street of the village of Santa Rosa. Muskets roared and amid the acrid smoke of royalist canon the Mexican troops fell. Heading the Spanish column was a priest who obscenely flapped his black cassock at the Mexicans just as warriors have done since the time ancient Scottish clansman lifted their kilts toward the hated English and Roman Legionnaires exposed their private parts to the enemy. The ragtag Mexican army retreated with its wounded but later returned to valiantly engage the enemy. The Mexican soldiers had blackened their faces with charcoal to give witness that he or she was not a Spanish sympathizer but, instead, was fighting for the independence of the homeland, the honor of the village, and the glory of the patron saint, Santa Rosa. Yes, there were women soldiers in this battle. Dressed in long skirts and colorful bandanas, they fought alongside the men. The Mexicans stormed back crying, "Viva Mexico, Viva Mexico, Viva Mexico!" Firing and reloading their muskets they advanced on the Spanish. Many fell on both sides, each side ultimately retreating to tend to the wounded and dying.

Why were the Spanish fighting a battle in this tiny village? Could it have been that all the charcoal in the province of Guanajuato came from Santa Rosa and the army that controlled this black gold would be the army that didn't freeze to death and could eat cooked beans? Could it have been that this village, situated on the continental divide, held a strategic position—the heights—on the Royal Highway leading to the fabled gold and silver mines of Valenciana?

The battle continued well into the afternoon but took a vital turn when the Mexican cavalry arrived and charged down on the brave, but now overpowered,

Spanish fusiliers. The Spanish retreated wearily to a hilltop with the equally fatigued but now victorious Mexicans in pursuit. As General Lee said to General Longstreet, "It is well that war is so terrible lest we grow fond of it." At this point everyone, friend and foe, sat down for a picnic as the re-enactment of the battle of Santa Rosa had come to an end.

We saw it all, and while I have seen re-enactment battles of the American Civil War on TV, I have never witnessed one in person, or as in this event, been right there among the troops. Yes, we ran for cover to avoid becoming a casualty from the cavalry charges. We held our hands over our ears as cannon fuses were lit and fired right next to us. We wondered how it was possible that any battle had ever taken place in Santa Rosa.

Let me explain. Santa Rosa is a small village located in the Sierra Guanajuato Mountains resting on the continental divide. It's about fifteen miles east of Guanajuato and not likely to be a candidate for this year's "Tidy Village" award. About the only thing of economic value produced in Santa Rosa is charcoal made from wood gathered in the great surrounding forests, ceramic plates and jugs, and baby boys, who grow up to work in the gold and silver mines of Guanajuato. The main street where the battle was fought is just about the only street in town. It is long, unusually straight for these parts, and is lined with a jumble of houses and shops. Why would Royalist troops choose this place to attack? Ah, but whoever said War had to make sense?

During the afternoon there was a break for speeches. A woman spoke accompanied by her venerable grandfather who was dressed in natural-colored muslin and a huge *charo* hat. He had a yellowed beard and walrus mustache indicative of his impressive age. Hollywood couldn't have done it better. It was hard to understand what the woman said, but the gist of the speech was that all the wars and revolutions of Mexico had a battle in Santa Rosa, and the Santa Rosarians always prevailed. Viva Mexico! Viva Santa Rosa!

Trip to the Pacific Beaches

It's mid-January and the Guanajuato nights have been unseasonably chilly; a trip to the beach for a few days would allow us to soak up the sun and provide a break from our intense schedule. We asked Jim and June Jackson, our next door neighbors, and Ron Mann and Sandra Ward to join us. A long day's drive took us to La Posada, a small beachside inn in Manzanillo, Mexico situated on the Pacific Ocean 168 highway miles south of Puerta Vallarta in the State of Colima.

The trip to Manzanillo took us past the Colima Volcano, which is 13,440 feet above sea level. Its last eruption was January 5, 1999, just twelve days prior to our trip. (You can see how Carole and I are keeping you abreast of the latest happenings in Mexico.) We could see a column of white smoke emanating from the peak as well as lava flows capping the upper tip of the mountain. Majestic and quite beautiful, the Colima Volcano left us with a feeling of awe and some apprehension, although on this January day, it quietly allowed us to pass. One had the feeling that *Volcan Colima* would one day have the last word with any who came too close.

We arrived at La Posada, climbed into our swimming suits and tried out the beach—sandy, clean, and blessed with gently rolling, warmly inviting waves. A German lady, Inga, and her husband, an ex-World War II U.S. bomber pilot, own The Posada. How they ended up in Mazanillo, Mexico, we didn't learn; but we did hear about and saw posters of Inga when she had been a ballet dancer and professional ice skater with the Ice Capades. La Posada was not a fancy place, but was clean, very comfortable, with a friendly ambience that made us all feel we would like to return some day. A fair amount of our short stay seemed to be devoted to determining where we would have our next meal. One exceptional dinner was spent at a restaurant named: "El Bigote," and although we had reservations about any restaurant that would so blatantly profess its narrow-minded intolerance, we went there anyway. I later learned that *"El Bigote"* meant "The Moustache," and not bigot, so I guess it was okay. The meal was memorable. Our table was open-air facing the ocean. While waiting for our meal to arrive, we watched an orange sunset so large it looked fake. All in our party proclaimed their orders of red snapper, sea bass and fresh and cooked oysters to be excellent. Our meal ended with music from some strolling *mariachis*.

I don't think it is possible to visit Manzanillo without seeing *Las Hadas*, a resort/hotel built in the late 1960's by a Bolivian tin magnate for $35 million. With its chalky domes, ice cream spires, Arabic arches and Eastern statuary, it is an exotic mixture of Moorish, Mediterranean, and Mexican architecture. It may be what Disney would have built if he didn't have a corporate board watching the bottom line. We stopped at Las Hadas for a drink, and after passing up a huge piano bar where the music was too loud and not very good, we went to a patio bar to listen to some guitarists who also played too loud and not very well. We finally settled on a beach bar with dance floor. The band was okay if you like ChaChaCha music. Please keep in mind that rooms without a view at Las Hadas cost $200 a night, but if you are not trying to economize you can stay in the Presidential suite for $2000 a night. I enjoyed watching the wealthy Americans dance but felt envious—it was not that they were rich, they were also so damn young and attractive. But who among us would ever want to be rich, young, beautiful—and tasteless?

We decided to break up the return trip to Guanajuato with an overnight stay at Mazamitla, a town the Jackson's had previously visited. Tucked away in the highlands of the State of Michoacan, this town of 11,000 people looked like a little piece of Switzerland. The inn where we stayed is called *"La Alpina."* The afternoon was spent walking around town and shopping for preserved fruit, a big item in Mazamitla. By the time we found the restaurant recommended to us it was closing time, but the sole waiter kindly let us in to wait while he conferred with the owner to see if it was okay to serve us. The waiter then checked with the cooking staff, three women who were already completing their day's final clean up. I heard the waiter ask the women something. They replied *"Si,"* and turning to me, they gave me a big smile. We had a fine meal. but I think the best part were the smiles and cheerful willingness to serve us even after the cooks had finished cleaning their pots and pans and had put everything away. We left a separate tip for the three women. I only mention this lest you think we are ungrateful slobs.

15

March 1999

Guanajuato and the Y2K Problem

It seems that none of us is able to escape the Y2K problem. I don't mean the actual problem that is supposed to occur next January 1. No, what I mean is the entire furor over this coming event. Now that the Clinton thing has been put to bed, so to speak, what we mainly hear on our satellite TV are reports of the impending disaster. I checked it out on the Internet and wow, if you believe what they say, you had better start buying canned food, water, a portable toilet, take all your money out of the bank, sell off any investments you have, buy some guns and ammunition, head for some remote spot on the earth and wait it out. It's that "remote spot" phrase that caught my attention because that's the kind of place where we happen to live.

Now to be sure, Guanajuato has plenty of computers and it seems by the number of computer training schools, that everyone here is learning how to use or program a computer. It is very common to go into a business place where the clerk will make a receipt on the computer, but when you go to pay, you will be asked, "Do you have the exact change?" If you don't have the correct *cambio* the clerk will reach into an old wooden cash box and with a combination of money from the cash box and <u>his pocket</u> give you your change within a few pennies. What I am trying to convey is that Guanajuato has a way to go before it is totally computer dependent. In contrast to what appears to be occurring in the United States, no one seems to be worried about the year 2000 computer glitch. You don't hear a lot of people talking about it.

I have an idea on why this might be the case. Given that everything seems to be about fifty to 100 years behind the times here, the Y2K problem is not likely to show up until at least the year 2050 or 2100. If you are one of those concerned about what might happen and feel you must go to some safe haven, well, we can put up a few people in our house, but just make sure that your flight is not scheduled for 1/1/2000.

A Trip to Michoacan

We had been talking to our neighbors, Jim and June Jackson, for several weeks about making a trip to Michoacan to see the monarch butterfly preserve and to visit a few spots in the area. It's been said that if you ask a Mexican, what is the most beautiful state in the country he will naturally say the state he comes from. But if you ask, "Well, besides your state?" he will probably say, Michoacan. The state of Michoacan is directly south of the state of Guanajuato so it is all within reasonable driving distance from where we live and next to Guanajuato it is about the prettiest state you will find in Mexico. We started our little four-day adventure by driving to Queretero to renew the sticker on our American licensed van. From there we soon entered Michoacan.

Butterfly Preserve at Angangueo

Like most people, I don't have a fondness for insects. Somewhere I read though, that if you divide insects into three groups you can begin to appreciate them more. At one end you have venomous spiders, scorpions, mosquitoes, and bees—insects that bite us. You don't have to like them. Appreciating these types requires a more advanced level of bugology best left to experts and other weird people. On the other end, you have butterflies, ladybugs, dragonflies, and other friendly insects that most of us can enjoy. Then, in the middle, you have many insects that don't particularly harm us but we don't care to have around. It is the butterfly, with its lilting name, which sounds for all the world like flutter-by, that is my favorite.

The wintering site of the monarch butterfly is about a one-hour five-mile ride up the *Sierra de Angangueo* Mountains from the town of Angangueo. We found a hotel, El Don Bruno, on the main street of this one street town. At 10,000 feet, the night and morning air is more than crisp. Our room had a *chiminea* (fireplace) and when we were ready to turn in a young man built us a roaring fire.

Carole, who was suffering from a terrible cold throughout the trip, finally got warm that evening.

Mining continues to be the town's principal activity but at a reduced pace than years past. We learned that during a labor management dispute some years ago, the managers (foreign, but nationality not mentioned) had intentionally caused a mine cave-in killing a number of miners. A monument was built honoring the miners who died. The managers, for their efforts, probably received the "Lifetime Achievement Award" from the Academy of Hard Ball Management.

The evening before we went to visit the preserve, I met Enrique, who operated a pickup truck service taking visitors up the mountain. The fee was $20 round trip for the whole load. The next morning as we were waiting to get assembled for our trip up the mountain I ran into two Mexican women, a mother and her daughter who were staying at the same hotel. They asked if they could share the truck ride with us and I said sure.

Enrique and his family operate three trucks but ours was the only one that had an enclosed bed. After we all climbed in a boy came around selling surgical masks at ten cents each. "What are these for?" we asked. Enrique explained, "It can get a little dusty where we are going." We were glad that we had the enclosed truck, the masks, and that we were among the first to visit the preserve this day. Later a fine powdery dust would rise from the school busses and from the little feet of battalions of children pounding the path on their way up the mountain. The road was rocky and curvy and although it was difficult to see out of the dusty windows, the scenery was breathtaking. Steep hillsides were terraced and contour planted—hard to imagine how they farmed this land without falling off.

June introduced her husband to our two fellow travelers as Diego that is the Spanish equivalent of James, I was Carlos and Carole was Caróle. Jim and I were later awarded the titles of San Diego and San Carlos for reasons that now escape me. The mother, Maria Solis and her daughter, Guadelope Cardona Solis, were from Mexico City. Maria who looked like she was in her early fifties, said she didn't work; she was a housewife. (Groans of protest from Carole and June.) Guadalupe, who was very trim and nice looking and looked about twenty-four or so, said she was an accountant. As we talked more, the mother said her daughter was a second lieutenant in the Mexican army serving in the Department of Defense. Later she added that her daughter had a brown belt in Karate, had entered competitions in Guatemala as well as Mexico, ran ten kilometers several days a week, and was an excellent swimmer. The mother explained that she was widowed and that while her husband was alive they had a second home in Puerto Vallarta. When our truck arrived at the monarch information center, Enrique, our driver said we could take all the time we wanted—he would wait for us. He explained that the entrance fee was $1.50, and that a guide at no cost would accompany us, but if we liked, we could give him a tip. Considering that the hotel was $40 for a double and the truck ride only cost $3.33 per person, a visit to the monarch sanctuary is certainly an economical excursion.

Our guide introduced himself, "Guadelupo Perfecto, at your service," he said. It seems to me, having a name like Perfecto must be quite a burden growing up. Although an old man, Perfecto seemed to be walking at a deliberately slow pace all the while we were huffing and puffing to keep up with him on our climb to the monarchs. This was our first encounter with an *oyamel* forest. The trees look similar to Douglas fir only with less foliage and all of it near the top. They rise to the height of a twelve-story building. High up in the trees you could see hoards of butterflies hanging onto the foliage. Wings folded together, the aggregation of butterflies appeared as a dark gray mass. Even though it takes fifty butterflies to weigh an ounce, the butterfly-laden branches were bent straight down from the weight. The day was partly cloudy and when the sun emerged from the clouds thousands of strikingly colored monarchs started to fly, a joyous and magical event to witness.

As Perfecto led us up the path he would stop to pick up fallen butterflies, some dead, and some hindered by the fine dust on their delicate wings. He set them on plant leaves just off the path or lofted them into the air. Probably only a few would survive but his picking them up seemed to reflect a sensitive appreciation for the insects—least of all, not to be walked on. Soon we were all picking up butterflies. I asked him if the government owned this preserve and he told me that it belonged to his *ejido,* which is the communal land of a group of indigenous people. It was they who decided how to run the preserve. Before visiting Angangueo I had the impression that the monarchs were in danger of loosing their habitat and that the Indians were cutting down the trees, lacking other resources. My impression changed as I saw the regulations they imposed to protect the monarchs. Stay on the path, no pets allowed, don't pick any plants, don't make any loud noises to try to stir up the butterflies, no flash pictures that might disturb these insects, and the list went on. The *ejidatarios* make a modest income from the entrance fee and from the selling of food and trinkets to people who come to visit the preserve. But even if the butterflies had no economic value I don't think they would knowingly hurt these lovely creatures. (I have since learned that there are other monarch wintering places in Michoacan and am unable to say if the butterflies are faring as well as at Angangueo.)

Biologists didn't discover the wintering site of the monarchs until 1975. I bet the Indians knew it all the time. Wintering in Mexico from November through March, the monarchs come from the upper mid-west and Canada, where they live on milkweed. The butterflies that come here are third generation of those that left to go north. How the grandchildren of the insects that flew north manage such a lengthy migration from dispersed sites to this specific wintering place is hard to fathom.

On the bumpy truck ride down I mentioned to Maria and Guadalupe that we would be driving down to Ciudad Hidalgo and from there we were going up to the hot spring baths of Los Azufres. Would they like a ride? Guadalupe was going to be a bridesmaid at a wedding the next evening in Mexico City but after a few moments of calculation, she said, "Yes, they would like to join us. It doesn't seem possible that this teeming metropolis, one of the world's largest cities, could be a mere two-hour bus ride away from this exquisite wilderness."

Los Azufres Spa and Geo-thermal Zone

The road from Ciudad Hidalgo to the spa was longer than we expected. The drive was through an *oyamel* forest that has to be among the finest forests in the world. I've seen the redwoods in California and this is certainly their equal. We finally reached the Azufres Spa and Camp Grounds at about 5 p.m. The receptionist said that there was only one vacant *cabaña* but it had three rooms, and three beds. Never mind that one bed was in the kitchen/dining area, we took it. Our charming and good-natured Mexican friends, Marie and Guadalupe, were now practically family, so we shared the *cabaña*.

Although it was cold outside we quickly got into our swimsuits and jumped into the large hot pool. Carole, whose cold had not let up, got into her swimsuit and winter jacket, and as she went down to the pool, kept mumbling, "What's wrong with this picture?" The pool was surrounded by *oyamel* trees about 140 feet tall so that as you looked up you saw a tiny patch of blue sky the size of the pool. We soaked and soaked. Sitting in these warm curative waters in the cold air gave me the sudden urge to put my hand on Carole's forehead and yell: HEAL! Didn't work.

There was a little store where we bought some eggs and canned refried beans that Maria cooked up, and with some food we had brought along, Guadalupe made a fine presentation out of our meager fare. San Diego was able to light the fireplace and we enjoyed our meal with some premixed cocktails, which I, San Carlos, had miraculously remembered to bring along. *Salud!*

At about 8 p.m. we heard a strange noise, which sounded like a steady downpour, only it wasn't raining. We went to bed with this loud "shhhh" sound continuing. Next morning as we started to leave we saw a large pressure tank apparatus with a ganglia of pipes, valves, and tubes, and steam leaking out. Our spa was the site of one of the Azufres geothermal mini-power generating units and the noise we heard was the escaping steam of a geyser.

In January of this year, the Mexican government announced that it was opening bidding on five new power projects with a total generating capacity of 2,800 megawatts worth an estimated $2.1 billion. The smallest of these is a 100-megawatt geothermal plant at Los Azufres in Michoacan. Geothermal, along with wind power, is considered to be environmentally the most desirable form of electric power generation and it is nice that Mexico has this potential.

We came down the mountain on Friday and saw Maria and Guadalupe off on the bus to Mexico City. Our destination was to another hot spring spa at a town called Zinapécuaro. We found a grand place called Atzimba where we had a big breakfast. The hotel looked down on a series of pools including a large one designed for a wave-making machine. Unfortunately, except for one small pool, they all lacked water. The receptionist said that the water was *tybia,* tepid. I asked if there was someplace where we could find a good hot thermal spa and she answered yes, there was a nice spa at the nearby town of Araró. She said there was a festival going on there at this time but we could probably find a room at the hotel. Festivals are just our ticket so off we went.

Festival de San Buenaventura de las Aguas Calientes de Aroró

A narrow road led us from Mexico Highway 120 toward the center of town. As we came over a small hill we could see vehicular traffic for miles and a steady stream of people walking. We could also see a bus staging area with several hundred tour busses. We continued on at a crawl until we found a policeman directing traffic; actually I believe he was shunting all the traffic on to a huge field away from the town. I spoke with the officer and told him we wanted to go to the hotel in town, so he waved us through. This was a little bit like rejecting the last lifeboat on the Titanic and insisting on a better one. Almost immediately we found ourselves completely traffic bound.

We didn't know it at the time, but learned later that the Festival of Aroró is 400 years old. The church contains an image of Christ formed from a rare mixture of cane and orchid pulp and is believed by the faithful to have caused miracles through the ages. Tens of thousands of people from all over Mexico were here for the festival and we were among them. Having been given permission to head directly into town we found ourselves in a long line of halted vehicles. The extraordinary patience of Mexicans was once again displayed. Almost everyone took the gridlock in stride. After a long wait we slowly made our way to a road which gave us a back exit from the town without ever getting close to the hotel spa, or the center of town. As we entered the next little town we encountered something we have never before seen in a Mexican town. Except for an old man sitting on a doorstep and a small boy playing in the street, the town was deserted. Everyone else it appeared had gone to Aroró.

We now found ourselves driving along the lacustrine flats on the south shore of Lake Cuitzio, which is about 34 miles long. Our goal was the town of Cuitzio, which except for an impressive convent and church proved to be a disappointment, so we drove on to Patzcuaro. This is one of the colonial gems of Mexico and deserving of a longer stay. Arriving late in the afternoon, we checked in at the hotel San Fernando on the main plaza and did some frenzied shopping.

Patzcuaro

In the 16th Century, a Spanish missionary, Vasco de Quiroga, founded and built the city of Patzcuaro. The creative talents of the artists who excel at ceramics, carvings, textiles, and the use of copper complement its beautiful architecture and town design. Quiroga who was impressed with Thomas Moore's ideas of utopian communities. He encouraged individual villages to specialize in a particular occupation and he introduced new handicrafts and methods from Spain. Today, one can notice that villages in the area continue to specialize in the making of certain crafts.

The Twin Pyramids of Cucuchucho

On the way to Tzintzuntzán from Patzcuaro we traveled a few miles to the pyramids near Cucuchucho. Don't you love the names of these towns? Too bad they don't have a railroad running through there. Could be the Cucuchucho, Tzintzuntzán and Western. The site has a small visitor's center and a guide to explain what you are seeing. There is a depressed courtyard or parade grounds, measuring about 200 feet by 400 feet in front of two identical truncated pyramids. The guide explained that archeologists had identified one pyramid as representing the sun and the other the moon.

Now I happen to be of the belief that archeologists spend too much time in the sun and whenever they are clueless in identifying some monument they come up with a religious interpretation. A thousand years from now some archeologist is going to identify the broken ruins of the Statue of Liberty as some kind of goddess that earthlings worshipped. Or, on discovering the small twin garages used for garaging his-and-her golf carts that I once saw in an Arkansas retirement community (I'm not kidding, I really saw these), the archeologists are going to claim that these structures represented the sun and the moon deities which earthlings revered.

I am preparing to write a scientific paper, the title of which is: *The Twin Truncated Pyramids of Cucuchucho and the Nagging Wife Phenomenon.* My take on this is that some Tarascan chief started to build a regular pyramid and his wife began to nag him about needing a pyramid of her own. So instead of completing his pyramid to the apex, he acquiesced and built a second truncated pyramid. Now, everyone was happy.

16

June 1999

What do You Call a Truckload of Girls?

The Sunday before Easter, I was driving into town and encountered heavy traffic on Avenida Miguel Hidalgo, the attractive entryway into the city. I found myself barely crawling along behind a 4 × 6 truck. Loaded in the back of the truck were nine or ten girls of thirteen to sixteen years old sitting on several blankets. In Mexico, it is not uncommon to see the cargo areas of all sizes of trucks loaded with human cargo. Mom and dad ride up in front with a toddler, a baby on Mama's lap, and a bunch of older kids and friends in the back of the truck. As traffic came to a halt, I noticed that the girls were playing some sort of game that seemed to be a lot of fun. They would laugh and giggle and would suddenly pile on top of one other forming a human pyramid perhaps four bodies high. The girls were pretty and the bodies looked soft and nubile, so I guess I have to admit I vicariously enjoyed this game, as well. When I was a kid, I think we played a game like this. It was called King of the Hill, or maybe just Pile-On, although at the time, I don't recall it involving 16-year-old girls. The group of girls I was watching did this over and over again until one of them got a nosebleed. The nosebleed brought the game to an end although not the smiling and laughing. Later I learned from the young women in the conversational English class that Carole and I tutor at the University that the name of this game is *"Manañitas Caliente,"* which means, "Hot Little Hands." I didn't inquire further as to why the game is called "Hot Little Hands"; I prefer to leave this bit of information to my imagination. I guess an event like this would never be written up in any visitor's guide, but I find it's the kind of thing that makes this place so delightful.

Back around 1950, I recall reading an article in the *Milwaukee Journal* that analyzed pleasure. (Incidentally, the *Milwaukee Journal* was at one time one of America's best newspapers until they shamefully took an editorial stand against early retirement for Wisconsin state and local government employees.) Anyway, the part I remember most about this article is that people feel the greatest pleasure in small things—a lot of small or frequent pleasures, rather than just one really big thing. That's one of the reasons I enjoy Guanajuato so much; there are a lot of little things that are interesting or that bring delight to a person living here.

So, shouldn't a truckload of girls have a more apropos name than simply a truckload of girls? How about a Gaggle of Girls? This has the right alliteration but it has already been used...as in gaggle of geese; besides, there is no real connection between the words gaggle and girls. Well, then, how about a Squeal of Girls; a Giggle of Girls? Oh, I think that's perfect!

The Collective Noun

Shortly after writing "What Do You Call a Truckload of Girls?" I came across an interesting page on the Internet called "The Collective Noun." These are defined as nouns that "denote a collection of persons or things regarded as a unit," such as a pride of lions, a covey of quail, a gaggle of geese, a charm of finches. The web page contained an extensive list of long-known collective nouns as well as new submissions. I was surprised to see that "a giggle of girls" had already been suggested, so I can't claim to be the originator. But here are a few of the new submissions that amused me:

An absence of waiters
An addition of mathematicians
A billow of smokers
A blaze of pyromaniacs
A brace of orthodontists
A clutch of testicles
A disputation of lawyers
A drove of cabbies
An embarrassment of parents
A flunk of students
A fold of chairs
A galaxy of starlets

A greed of lawyers
A gross of farts
A hassle of errands
A jam of tarts
A kettle of drums
A mass of Catholics
An order of waiters
A pander of toadies
A pinhead of angels
A pink of liberals
A prey of nuns
A quarrel of lawyers
A shortage of dwarves
A slice of circumcisions
A sulk of teenagers
And finally,
A whored of prostitutes

Check out The Collective Noun web page at: http://www.ojohaven.com/collectives/ You may want to try your hand at creating a collective noun. I have already submitted: A pickle of fines, a pride of ownerships, and a dust-off of plans.

Trip to Tlaxcala

Our friends, Nancy Fennema and Marti Cutler were visiting us, and we thought it would be fun to take to the waters, as they say, at our favorite thermal spa, *La Gruta*, in San Miguel. There were probably eight others in the spa that day: a German mother with two children, an older man with a young knockout Mexican woman, and a few Americans. Marti and I were enjoying a cold glass of dark Mexican beer as we soaked in the warm waters when I overheard the Americans talking about a charming town they had run into in Mexico. The place was called "La Scala" they said. It had only about 60,000 people but was the capital of the State of the same name, which they identified as being the smallest state in Mexico. They went on to say that "La Scala" was a beautiful Mexican colonial city, very clean and neat, located about 22 miles north of the city of Puebla. You could buy a four bedroom colonial house with a walled garden and many other features for about $57,000 U.S. They described the climate as a little bit colder than Guanajuato in the winter because it is at a higher elevation. Still, "La Scala" has many similarities with Guanajuato, they said. For one thing, it has an amazing history—pre-Hispanic, Colonial, and Mexican.

I thought I knew the names of all the states in Mexico but I had never heard of a state or town named "La Scala." La Scala, I thought, was supposed to be an opera house in Milan, Italy. The town they described sounded intriguing, so I checked our atlas after returning home. What I found located north and near Puebla were a number of towns with Indian names such as Apizaco, Cacaxtla, Tlaxcala, and the like. It finally dawned on me that the "T" in "Tla" is pronounced so softly that it sounds almost the same as "la", and that the "x" is pronounced like an "s"; the name Tlaxcala sounds very much like La Scala, but has nothing to do with Italian opera houses.

Shortly after our visit to *La Gruta*, I attended a meeting of The Friends of the Alhondiga Museum, a group we belong to. The director announced that they were planning a trip to a place that sounded like La Scala, only this time I knew it was Tlaxcala. Carole and I eagerly signed up for this three-day, two-night excursion, all for $120US per person including bus transportation, hotel, meals, and a couple of congenial *horas de amigos,* (happy hours) where they pour some tequila and rum drinks and everybody sings romantic songs of Mexico. The trip took us through Queretero, Mexico City, and on into Tlaxcala.

The Tlaxcalteca Indians battled Cortez, but later joined with the Spanish to fight against the Aztecs, their historic enemies. It is generally conceded that Cortez didn't have a chance against the Aztecs save for the fact that he was able to get help from the Tlaxcaltecas. Because of heavy tribute imposed on them by the Aztecs, the Tlaxcaltecas were in constant war with the Aztecs and welcomed the opportunity to join with the Spanish. As a reward for their help, Cortez granted the Tlaxcaltecas permanent exemption from Spanish taxes, sort of an early day Proposition 113. After the conquest and during the colonization of New Spain, the Tlaxcaltecas, who were exceptionally fine artisans, accompanied the Spaniards building their towns and pacifying hostile Indians. The book, *Don Diego de Montemayor*, mentions how my ancestor, who founded the city of Monterrey, Mexico, brought 400 Tlaxcalteca Indians and their wives with him to Monterrey. Led by Franciscan friars, they helped build the city. They also were vital in the pacification of hostile Indians who occupied the area. I might add, that according to the book, "The Indians that helped build Monterrey were given good land, and in a location they preferred."

The guide of the Alhondiga group, Rafael Juarez Martinez, had been studying for three years to be a government-certified guide, and he had one more year to go before completing his studies. Archeology, anthropology, geology, history, economics, sociology, architecture—there was no aspect of Tlaxcala that he could not explain in depth. We visited the Franciscan Convent of Our Lady of the Assumption in the historic center of town. (Now, I find myself getting a little out of my range of knowledge here, and so perhaps our good friend Father Bill Hower, back in Columbus, Wisconsin, could assist in case my information is faulty on the Assumption.) Although we were not able to visit the nearby town of Huamantla, I was fascinated by what I learned on the Internet about this town's mid-August feast of the Assumption.

The convent, a magnificent structure, was started in 1527 and named after the Assumption. It contains a large stone baptismal font that was used by the four noble Tlaxcaltecan lords who Cortez brought into the faith; it is still in use today. It includes a spacious walled courtyard with a large belfry detached from the church near a three-arched entrance. We heard the bells chiming frequently during our visit. The sound was clear; the tone was deep and very loud. Rafael said that people in Puebla, twenty-two miles to the south, believed they could hear the bells of *Nuestra Señora de la Asunción*. Actually, there was a string of villages that would ring their bells successively when the big bells of *Nuestra Señora* started to ring.

Tlaxcala is an elegant little city that hasn't yet been discovered by Americans and Canadians. One of the members of our tour group told us that she visited the public market and was amazed at how clean it was. She learned that they have a rule which is strictly enforced: any owner of a stall who fails to pick up litter surrounding his stand is fined twenty pesos on the spot. Another thing we noticed is that nowhere did homes or businesses use broken glass on the top of walls, which is pretty standard throughout Mexico as a deterrent to *rateros* (robbers) climbing over the walls. The state of Tlaxcala has only 880,000 people and is also small in area—only 1,550 square miles, about the size of Dane County, Wisconsin where I served as Planning Director. Another difference is that Dane County doesn't have Malinche, a 14,100-ft. mountain located within the state of Tlaxcala.

As I visit various places in Mexico. I often wonder if some of the people I meet or see on the streets look like the original people whom the Spanish encountered. As you visit different parts of Mexico, you can observe regional differences in the physical appearance of the people. In Tlaxcala, we saw many people who were graced with very fine, almost delicate, features. Our guide, Rafeal, resembled many others we saw here. There is a pre-Hispanic image made of gold that is often used to symbolize Mexico in tourist brochures. It is the figure of a man or deity, having a broad face with delicate features and protruding and slightly pointy ears. It's a friendly face, almost a happy face, somewhat of a cross between

Alfred E. Neuman of *Mad Magazine* and Ross Perot, except not as goofy looking as Perot. I was taken back when I realized that our guide resembled this statue. But what should one expect, George W. Bush, Jr.?

Tlaxcala is laid out along classic Spanish colonial town-planning principles—it has large rectangular blocks with a large central plaza that has governmental buildings on one side, a church on another, and an arcade of shops on a third side. On a fourth side were some old stone buildings. Rafael pointed out one large building that had been the home and office of a wealthy and prominent attorney who owned many rental properties. He collected rents from people who could afford to pay, but from those who could not pay, all he asked of them was a contribution of a stone for the front of his building. Those "contributions" grew into the fine façade that stands today.

The constancy in the layout of towns throughout Latin America is a result of the Law of the Indies, which among other things, defined in precise terms how a colonial town was to be built. This same set of laws set forth the rights of the indigenous people. It is interesting to me that the Law of the Indies could be so scrupulously followed with respect to city planning and so flagrantly ignored and violated with respect to the rights of the people. While the Spanish Crown had a real concern with the way the Indians were being treated, the conquistadors believed that they had earned the right to exploit both the people as well as the land. *Hidalgos* is what they wanted to be—Spanish gentlemen who never had to work.

Among many of Tlaxcala's outstanding attractions are the murals in the Palace of Government, a building constructed in the 1500's but later updated, in part, to include very elegant parlors reflecting the French influence that began in the 1860's. The murals cover 5,000 square feet of area and portray the complete history of Tlaxcala, from ancient Olmec civilizations up to and including depictions of American flags and slogans such as "Manifest Destiny" and "America for the Americans." In his presentation on the murals, our guide treated this part very lightly, and although I was prepared to grab Carole and beat a hasty retreat, none of the forty or so Mexicans on the tour even gave us a dirty look. I can only assume that none of them could read the foot-tall English words.

About ten miles from Tlaxcala is the archeological zone of Cacaxla. There were several pyramids including one that we climbed, a ziggurat circular shape when viewed from the top, and comprised of a spiral ramp. Had Frank Lloyd Wright designed New York's Guggenheim Museum using this pyramid as a prototype, he got the shape right, but he built it upside down.

As we climbed various other pyramids, we were able to see an enormous structure about a mile away—it appeared to be a huge roof covering a small city. Later, our bus took us to within half a mile of this site, at which point we walked in to visit the ruin. Covering the site is a roof of an unusual design that I would estimate was at least 500 x 1,000 feet with no structural supports except at the periphery and using steel cables to hold the whole thing up. In response to a question about this structure, our guide explained that a Monterrey construction company using Japanese technology had built the edifice. We were permitted to visit the dig but we had to walk on special platforms protecting the site. What we saw was an enclave where ancient Cacaxtlan nobility had lived. The exhibit was complete, even including pens for their birds. The outstanding feature of this site was its murals, some of them in remarkably good condition. In all the archeological zones we have visited in Mexico, we have been impressed with the quality of treatment and display. It is a good thing that Mexico excels in archeology as it has so much of it with only a small portion yet identified.

We next visited the church of Ocatlan. This church, like other buildings in Tlaxcala, had a unique style in which hexagonal clay tiles had been imbedded in cement on the building's façade to produce a distinctive design. It seems remarkable to me that a state as small as Tlaxcala can have its own architectural style and one so different from other parts of Mexico.

17

August 1999

More Collective Nouns, Trip to Queretaro, Trip to Bernal, Charreada, The Weather

More Collective Nouns

In the previous issue of letter from Mexico I had a little article on "The Collective Noun." Several readers sent in nominations for collective nouns, and while I am not the official depository for collective nouns, I am happy to pass along some of these submissions. From my sister, Bertha Burghard in Indianapolis, comes: A Brag of Boys or A Bluster of Boys. From Charles Towill, now in his summer home in Alaska: "We've just received your latest Letter and I've been wracking my shrunken brain for brilliant collective nouns. So far nothing much, but how about A Growl of Polar Bears, A Howl of Wolves, A Trunk of Elephants." (I like, A trunk of elephants.) From Bob Ficken in Madison comes A Fringe of Friars. From Don Peacock in Arizona comes this message: "How about A Bounty of Breasts to balance out your Clutch of Testicles." **(I would like to clarify a point, Don; this were not my Clutch of Testicles.)** There were more submissions but I can't remember at this moment where I put the letters, which suggests another collective noun: A Lapse of Oldsters.

Trip to Queretaro

We've been to Queretaro perhaps five or six times but never were able to see many of the sites mentioned in the travel books. Gus and Marina Garcia, from Austin, Texas, were visiting us and they were interested in seeing Queretaro, so we set off for the trip. After driving eighty-three miles east of Guanajuato on a four-lane divided highway we arrived in Queretaro in a couple of hours. In the center of town is the colonial district with its old mansions, historic buildings, monuments, and narrow streets some of which have been made into pedestrian walkways. On the periphery along an outer belt-line is a collection of industries with prominent American, European, as well as Mexican, names. What we learned is that the national government has been encouraging the dispersal of industry away from Mexico City; Queretaro is one of the chosen cities.

Our guide, Lydia, showed us the town and I was surprised to learn from her that Queretaro seems to have at least as many legends and just as much history as Guanajuato. For example we passed an attractive, very old bar that had a plaque in front explaining that it had been in business since 1847. The bar's name was *La Carambada*. The story goes that it was named after a legendary female stage-coach robber who was called *La Carambada*. Every time she robbed a coach she would open her blouse, exposing her ample breasts, and people would cry out, "*Hay, caramba!*"

We visited the "Hill of the Bells," infamous due to its being the place where the Emperor Maximilian was executed along with two of his top generals. It is interesting that the crowned heads of Europe pleaded with the Juarez government that his life be spared, while Lincoln, who was president at that time, did not support this amnesty. Maximilian, at least earlier, could actually have escaped and returned to Europe, but his Mother, in an outstanding example of filial love, exhorted him to stay and die among the people of his empire. Now I don't want to take sides on this long past issue, but what I would like to know is what was this royal Euro-trash doing over here in the first place?

The reason that this very elegant and sedate park is named "The Hill of the Bells" is not because there are any bells but rather that there is a large rock which, when hit sharply with another rock, makes the sound of a bell. We had an opportunity to "ring the rock" ourselves. During the battle against the imperialist forces, the Mexicans were surprised that some of their gunshots resulted in ringing sounds, not like the "Ziiing" from gunshots we use to hear in old cowboy movies, but a real "Clang."

Closer to the center of town is the large Convent of Santa Cruz. The sturdy walls of this convent were breached by Mexican canons—the opening still remains—permitting the Mexicans to enter the convent and capture Emperor Maximilian. The site of this same convent is where the Otomi Indians surrendered to the Spanish. One of the legends Lydia told us is that the Indians worked out an agreement with the Spanish that both sides would fight without the use of arms. This was clever of the Indians because they lacked the armament technology of the Spanish and they felt pretty certain that they could easily outfight the Spaniards *mano a mano*. But the Spanish knew that on the scheduled day of battle an eclipse would occur (hasn't this been used in several movies?); to add to the intrigue, the image of a saint miraculously appeared. Lydia didn't explain how they managed the saint trick, but the final score at the end of the day was Spaniards one, Indians zero.

Another legends of Queretero concerns two houses built side by side. The two owners got into a competition as to who could build the most beautiful house. Each kept adding to and elaborating his home. The competition went on until the city finally put a stop to it punishing one of the owners by requiring him to close off one of his balconies.

Across the plaza from this house is another fancy place where an eccentric owner believed he could fly and one day jumped off the roof of his house to prove it. His initials, *NPV*, still remain just below the cornice of the house. The folks of Queretaro said this stood for, *No Puede Volar,* or in English, "He Can't Fly."

There is much more to this fine city; someday you will have to come to Queretaro yourself.

Trip to Bernal

On our trip to Queretaro with Gus and Marina, we made a little side trip to the Village of Bernal. As we approached the village we began to see a huge monolithic protrusion appearing from otherwise flat ground. The Rock, or as it is known in Spanish, *La Roca* is a chunk of basalt that my guidebook tells me is second in size only to Ayers Rock in Australia. However, the folks in Bernal say it is third largest to The Rock of Gibraltar and Sugar Loaf Mountain in Rio de Janeiro. The village sits at the base of the rock, and the assent up the rock starts within Bernal. Carole and Marina were shopping in the little stores that sell needlework. I accompanied them for a while and was impressed with how exceptionally friendly and polite the clerks and shopkeepers are. Later, Gus and I began our climb up The Rock; I would have welcomed a push. I dropped out about a fourth of the way up where there were some stands selling cold drinks and mineral specimens. Gus continued further half way up where he found a church that the guidebook tells us houses a priest now too old to say mass. Judging by the climb he must have been there a long time. To reach the summit, which is well above the church, requires mountain climbing gear.

The town of Bernal is attractive, and we had a fine meal at La Escondida, an outdoor, roof-covered restaurant that if one sits in the right place affords a view of The Rock. We met someone who told us that every March 21, during the Spring Equinox, people from all over Mexico and even the United States come "to take in the energy emanating from the rock." Now I have seen the Texaco TV commercials where they show their geologists exploring the most remote and inhospitable parts of the planet, and if there were any energy to be had at *La Roca de Bernal,* you can bet that Texaco, Mobil and Shell would all be there.

Now, regarding the landing of UFO's and extra-terrestrials at Bernal, I'm afraid I am not permitted to discuss that

Charreada

A *charreada*, described as a Mexican rodeo, is probably a close cousin to a rodeo but really is in a different class. At least, in my opinion, it has a higher tone to it—they don't have any of those clowns. I suspect it is a rich man's sport in Mexico. For one thing, there is a special stadium built for this purpose. The stadium itself is circular in shape with the grandstands surrounding the rodeo "court." A track leading directly into the stadium allows the cowboys to enter the ring unencumbered by the stadium. The most striking difference of the Charreada is the costuming of the cowboys, *charros*, and cowgirls, *charras*. They wear elaborate costumes often ornately decorated with silver. Contrary to the U.S. Rodeo, the Charreada emphasizes riding skills rather than our emphasis on speed and competition.

Our neighbor, June Jackson, likes to ride horses and frequently goes to Faffi Romero's ranch a few miles outside of Guanajuato to avail herself of Faffi's generosity in letting friends and acquaintances ride her fine horses. Faffi is something of a legend around here because of her benevolence to a variety of causes primarily ones benefiting children. She is sometimes referred to as the "Paper Heiress," that's paper as in Kimberly-Clark. She has nine children all of whom I am told were born in Wisconsin. She is married to the recently retired rector of the University of Guanajuato and now candidate for governor.

One morning, June told us of a national *charreada* in Apaseo El Grande and asked if we would be interested in going. Apaseo is a town about fifty miles away from Guanajuato on the road to Queretaro. It has a wonderful array of baroque architecture plus a *charreada* ring. We arrived late but in time to see the end of the first session of the day's events. Outside the ring were stands selling ornate saddles and other tack, but what caught my eye, well actually my nose, was the aroma coming from a group of restaurants in a series of tents. The Jacksons, Carole, and I grabbed some seats at a long table and ordered a taco and beer. Shortly thereafter, as the restaurant filled, two Mexican couples came to our table, sat down and ordered a large platter of *carnitas*, which soon arrived. *Carnitas* are pieces of browned pork and are made by covering the meat with salted water, boiling the water away and continuing to cook the pork until all the fat has been rendered out. These tasty bits are served on a *tortilla* with *Salsa Cruda Mexicana* and are very delicious. They insisted that we share their *carnitas;* I think they ordered a kilo (2.2 pounds) so there was plenty to go around. They also ordered a bottle of tequila and practically filled my plastic cup. These were real *charreada* aficionados and they explained some of the finer points to us. One of the officials walked by and they asked him to join our table and introduced us to him. Later, when we returned to the ring we found two *señoritas* sitting in front of us. They were *charredas* from Apaseo El Grande who apparently had already performed and were now adorning the grandstands. June explained that as these young women rode, they would fan their large and colorful skirts over the backs of the horses.

The Weather

From what we've been watching about the hot weather in the States this July it seems almost cruel to report on weather conditions in Guanajuato. On a previous trip to Texas I bought a rain gauge and an electronic thermometer, the kind that records the last high and low outdoor temperature. I have been recording the weather since February and will share my findings along with multi-year data that I copied from a U.S. government publication that gives the monthly average temperature and inches of rainfall for Guanajuato. I suspect that there is a fair amount of variation in different locations around the city but my chart represents the conditions at our house, *Casa Colibrís*—Hummingbird House. It has always seemed to me rather meaningless to list an average temperature for a month, or even a day. Seventy-five degrees is a nice temperature, but if it is the average of 95 and 55 degrees you don't have a lot of comfort. For the months of February through July, my chart shows the average daily highs, the average daily lows as well as the average for the month, plus the highest and lowest temperatures for the month. The coldest it ever got was 55.8 in February; the warmest 83.1 in June, but overall, May is the warmest month of the year in Guanajuato. As you can see on the chart, there aren't a lot of extreme temperatures. Although the air is very dry and we don't suffer from humidity, the sun feels very warm and it is best to stay in the shade on a warm day and enjoy the cool air. On a winter day, when the temperature drops into the 50's or 60's, it is very pleasant to sit outdoors and soak up the sun. With such a moderate climate that has little variation it is surprising how one can still complain when it's two degrees from perfect. I think we may have brought with us this habit of complaining after living in the upper Midwest for so long.

1999 Weather								
Recorded by Charles Montemayor Guanajuato, GTO Mexico							Multi Year Data	
	Av. High	Av. Low	Overall Av.	High est	Lowest	Rain Inches	Temp.	Rain Inches
Feb.	68.5	62.4	65.4	71.1	55.8	0	59.7	0.31
Mar.	69.5	72.8	69.5	76.5	63.3	0	64.2	0.25
Apr.	74	77.8	74	81.9	64.4	0	68.2	0.23
May	80	72.2	76.1	82.6	67.6	7.1	70.5	1.08
June	77.7	70.8	74.3	83.1	68	1.4	68.2	5.37
July	71.2	73.6	68.8	79	65.7	5.7	65.8	6.54
6 Mo.						14.2		13.8

18

January 2000

What Does It Cost To Live in Mexico? Girl from Down Under Loses Bikini Top at La Gruta, The Lord Perfects Skin Pigmentation in Humans, You <u>Can</u> Take it with You, Public Works Report, Monts Get a Dog, House Gets Painted, Millennium Arrives in Guanajuato

What Does It Cost To Live in Mexico?

The truth is you can live pretty cheaply in Mexico although not as cheaply as some visitors believe. Conversely, it can also cost a lot depending on your needs and wants. I have seen some data that a middle-class Mexican family can live on U.S.$12,000 a year. This probably assumes they own their own home clear of any mortgage. Mortgage interest rates are so high in Mexico that few Mexicans can afford them. General living costs for Americans living in Mexico may be higher depending on the amount of imported items one needs or wants. For example, Mexico has some inexpensive delicious cheese that we enjoy, but we still like to buy some Wisconsin cheddar when we can get to Leon where they have American stores like Costco and Sam's Club. We pay more for these imported items, more here than were we to buy the same item in the U.S. Mexico imports manly from the U.S. but also from China, Taiwan, and other far-eastern countries the same items you see in the United States, but they are considerably more expensive here.

Food prices are cheaper at the two Guanajuato municipal markets than at the one available supermarket chain. It is hard to track the prices at the independent *mercados* because nothing is pre-packaged or price-marked. The shopkeeper weighs your purchase and calculates in his head how much you owe. I think they are completely honest in these places, but I am too embarrassed to ask the independent shopkeeper how much a half kilo of carrots or tomatoes cost—like I might not buy them if they were too high. The following table shows prices in

Guanajuato and in Beloit, Wisconsin. Most of the Mexican grocery items are from the Commercial Mexicana, which is a large grocery and dry goods store that has no competition in our town. The prices recorded have been updated to April 2002. They are expressed in U.S. dollars and have been converted from kilos to pounds where appropriate. Shopping at the Comercial Mexicana is convenient because they have parking on the store roof, but one pays for this convenience. For example, the price of tomatoes on the same day is 66 cents per pound at the Comercial and 25 cents at a little store one block away.

Based on figures found on a Web site, the same items in Guadalajara and the Lake Chapala region south of Guadalajara are cheaper than in Guanajuato. We have also noticed lower prices in nearby Silao and Irapuato. San Miguel de Allende, with its large ex-pat community, seems higher than Guanajuato. A consensus of a few of us Guanajuato gringos is that a couple can live comfortably here for $2,000US per month, exclusive of housing. In my opinion, I think it is a mistake to move to Mexico if the only reason you do so is the belief that it will cost less. First of all, it may not be as cheap as you imagined, but more importantly, you have to really love this country and her people if you are going to be happy here. You have to be able to laugh at the frustrations and inconveniences that are a part of this lifestyle. If you are a stressful person you may find your stress level abating, but conversely, depending on what stresses you out, living in Mexico could put you over the edge. Automobiles, appliances, electronics and most manufactured items are definitely more expensive here. Hand-made wood furniture and items from wrought iron or brass are less expensive. If you have an eye for design, the artisans can make your personally designed creation. You might have to wait awhile before it gets done, but the results are often very beautiful.

Cost Comparisons

	$U.S. GTO	$U.S. Wisc.		$U.S. GTO	$U.S. Wisc.
Telephone, basic service	20/mo.	13.56	Chicken, whole	1.00/lb.	1.38/lb
Telephone call to U.S.	1.04/min.		Chicken, legs	0.68/lb.	1.48/lb
Electricity, light, TV, stereo	73.60/mo.		Ground beef, lean	1.91/lb	2.28/lb

Cost Comparisons (Continued)

Gas: range, dryer, hot water	38.95/mo.		Pork chops	2.52/lb.	3.58/lb
Water, tap (Not drinking)	6.44/mo.		Eggs, dozen	1.07	0.59.
Drinking water, 4 gal. Jug	1.79		Rice, packaged	0.41/ lb.	0.55/lb
Haircut, man's	2.78	12.00.	Beans, packaged	0.72/ lb.	0.70/lb
Haircut, ladies	4.46	13.00	Bananas	0.32/ lb.	0.49/lb
Car wash	1.60		Mangos, Ataulfo	0.48/ lb.	0.89/ea.
Maid, 3 days/ wk.Cooks,			Oranges, Valencia	0.16/ lb.	0.75/lb
cleans, washes, irons	44.47/wk.		Grapefruit	0.21/ lb	0/50/ea
Gardener 3 days/ wk 3hr/day	16.62/wk.		Leaf lettuce	0.39	0.98.
Plumber/hour	16.36	68.00.	Avocado, Hass	0.60/ lb.	0.98 ea.
City bus	0.27		Onions, white	0.42/ lb	0.98/lb
Doctor office visit	11.11	68.00	Tomatoes, Roma	0.66/ lb.	2.19/lb
Doctor home visit	22.23	None	Potatoes, white	0.64/ lb.	0.59/lb
Dental, clean teeth by doctor	27.77	50.00	Squash, zucchini	0.60/ lb.	0.98/lb
3 BR Apartment/ mo.	167-556		Broccoli	0.52/ lb.	0.88/lb
Gasoline, unleaded	2.75/gal	1.45	Milk	0.78/ qt.	1.15/qt
Dinner 1st. class restaurant,			Margarine,	0.95/ lb.	1.09/lb
incl. wine and cocktail	22.23		Bread, white lg.	0.94	2.28

Cost Comparisons (Continued)

Dinner, med. class rest.		Coca Cola, 12 oz.	0.39	0.30
chicken dinner	5.96.	Ballentines, scotch ¾ ltr	21.00	29.99
Hamburger & fries in rest.	3.67	Beer, 6-pack	4.77	7.39
Dinner, inexpensive restaurant	2.78/ea.	Cat food, Whiskas	0.51	0.42
Newspaper, Eng. language	0.89/ea	Tomatoes, street	0.25/lb.	

Girl from Down Under Loses Bikini Top at La Gruta

A few months ago, I accompanied a couple male visitors to La Gruta, a favorite thermal water spa. While we were soaking up the therapeutic waters of Pool #2, a young blond woman approached us inquiring: "Has anyone seen my bikini top?" She went on to explain that she was visiting from Australia. We hadn't seen her bikini top—heck, we hadn't even seen her get out of the pool. I think this is something we would have all remembered!

I thought this an amusing anecdote and shared it with dinner guests, Betsy and Ed Schiff a few days later. Betsy and Ed live in New York City, and as such I assumed that they might be more worldly than I. Betsy quickly clued me in with the following: "I don't see how men can fall for a line like that." I have to admit that I actually took a quick look into Pool #3, which is a dark grotto, to see if I could find that bikini top. But then, you have to remember I'm always trying to be helpful.

The Lord Perfects Skin Pigmentation in Humans

In past *Letters from Mexico* I have commented on how physically attractive many Mexicans are, particularly the women. While the perception may be that all Mexicans have dark brown complexions, the fact is that they come in just about every color and shade—from blue-eyed, fair-skinned blondes to darker toned complexions and jet-black hair. It's true that most Mexicans (I've seen) have deeper brown complexions than most gringos, but there are a surprising number of variations. Once in a while you come across a young woman or man that has strikingly beautiful skin pigmentation—a light creamy brown, like *café au lait*.

I got to thinking about how this might have come about and imagined that St. Peter and the Lord were reflecting on the Lord's handiwork in determining human skin color. The conversation might have gone something like this:

The Lord: *Peter, I'm rather pleased with the nice skin tones I've given people.*

St. Peter: *You surely have done a fine piece of work there, Lord. You've got black, brown, red, yellow, and white. I particularly like your discretion in not making any blue, purple, or green people.*

The Lord: *Well, I prefer the earth tones or just an off-white.*

St. Peter: *You've worked hard and you deserve a little break. Here, have a cup of coffee. Do you take cream with that?*

The Lord: *Sure put a little cream in my coffee. Well, a little more. Say, isn't that a nice color? Let's make some people the color of that coffee. We'll put them in Latin America.*

St. Peter: *Whatever you say boss, but what's the standard for <u>that</u> tan color? There are a lot of browns and tans. I mean there's acorn, alesan, alazarin brown, antique bronze, Argos brown, autumn leaf, biscuit, Bismarck brown, bister, bone brown, bunny brown, burnt almond, burnt umber—well, the list of brown tones just keeps on going. Could you be a little more specific?*

The Lord: *I want these people to be the color of my coffee—rich coffee with a good dash of cream in it. And be sure to make them just dark enough so that you can't see any blue veins showing through. I hate those blue veins.*

St. Peter: *Consider it done. And what color of hair for these people?*

The Lord: *I want their hair to be black—real black.*

St. Peter: *And what's the standard for that black color you are looking for?*

Lord: *I want their hair to be as black and shiny as Monica Lewinski's.*

St. Peter: *Who's Monica Lewinski, I never heard of her?*

The Lord: *You will, you will!*

You <u>Can</u> Take it with You

There's always something interesting to catch your eye in Guanajuato. Seen on *Avenido Juarez:* a gray hearse moving down the street with a chrome luggage rack on top.

Public Works Report

It's time for our latest report on Guanajuato's public works and development projects. The new road development for Guanajuato's entrance and exit to the city is quite beautiful and makes coming into the city much easier. The construction involved building an additional two-lane entrance road that passes through two new tunnels. The old two-lane road that at one time carried all of the traffic to and from the city has been resurfaced and is now the exit from Guanajuato. The two divided highways merge at a new interchange designed with graceful, natural stone arches. I imagine that this is the only highway grade separation in the world that has been built entirely of stone, a most fitting design for this Spanish colonial city.

However, one on-ramp to the interchange, although safer than the at-grade crossing it replaced, requires special vigilance because of the acute angle at which it merges with the higher speed traffic. One must cross two lanes of oncoming traffic whose view is partially blocked by a [lovely] stone wall. Perhaps this is the reason that all the buses and many of the taxis have icons of the Virgin on the dashboard or hanging from the rear-view mirror.

Businessmen in the community are excited about a proposal to build a $10 million hotel complex and golf course. The development is planned to be located along the new entrance to Guanajuato on government-owned land. (Don't you love the way entrepreneurs are able to brilliantly discover hidden opportunities that lesser folks can barely imagine? It's like Donald Trump said: he is the only one really qualified to be President of the United States because he is the only one that has earned a billion dollars. Where do you suppose that leaves Abraham Lincoln? Step aside Donald; Bill Gates gets top billing now.) Anyway, presently, the nearest existing golf courses are in Leon and Irapuato. I have been told the developers hosted a grand *fiesta* for the faculty and students of the University of Guanajuato School of Architecture as well as the planning and development staff of the city in order to explain the project and display a beautiful development model.

Tourism is an important part of this city's economy, but presently the majority of incoming tourists are Mexican. "Tipping" the tourism scale to attract wealthy American and Japanese golfers could very well change the historic character of Guanajuato. I don't personally have anything against golfers, but golfing has never been a reason to visit Guanajuato. And even more importantly, the scarcity of water eight months of each year would be a big problem. I suppose I would feel differently about this project if I were a golfer, but I'm terribly concerned about the reality of a golf course here; so many projects get announced that never materialize. Once upon a time, a high-speed rail line was on the books and, too, a state-of-the-art, "finest in the world" industrial park built on the east side of the state. It's been a long time since we heard a lot of talk about these grand proposals.

There is one new development that is actually under construction. A Spanish consortium is building a *funicular* (cable car) to run from an area in back of the San Diego Church at the Jardin de Union in the center of town up a steep slope to the *Pipila* monument. *Pipila,* you will recall, was the legendary young Indian miner who used a flat stone as a shield to get to the front doors of the *Alhondiga de Granaditas* and set them on fire. This permitted the Mexican insurgents to storm the building and overtake the Spanish who were using the Alhondiga as their fortress. Pipila is a national hero and a very special hero to the people of Guanajuato.

At first, the idea of a cable car for Guanajuato struck me as a dumb idea. In my view, Guanajuato didn't need another tourist attraction. However, the plans include a restaurant to be built at the top, and the more I've thought about it, the better the concept. I like the idea of escorting visitors to the *Pipila* monument and enjoying a meal while overlooking the city. Just in case you don't have a *funicular* in your town, why don't you plan to visit us in Guanajuato?

Monts Get a Dog

Her name is Samantha. She came to us as a gift from Sandra Ward who had "received" her unannounced at her front door. Sandra's motto could well be "give a leg up for dogs" as she is tireless in her efforts to save strays—she takes them to the vet for R&R (rest and recuperation) and then places as many as she can in good homes.

Samantha was a pup when we got her, and we've watched her grow up to be one of the oldest puppies in dogdom. For some reason, Samantha doesn't want to mature. Every time I see her I think of Alan Greenspan's exhortation on the stock market, "irrational exuberance." She has learned not to jump directly on me, but instead, she jumps straight up and down. She wraps her muzzle around the leash in my hand twisting it around all the while jumping up and down. Mexican mothers, when they want there little kids to settle down, often yell *calma, calma*. I thought Samantha, having been born here, might respond to *calma, calma,* but it doesn't seem to work. The best I can do is to try the Mr. Rogers soft approach until she settles down sufficiently to hook her up on the leash.

Samantha is a nice looking dog; most of her coat is as black and shiny as Monica Lewinski's (the new standard), however, elegant she is not. Her proclivity for digging up our garden and potted plants leaves her nose caked with dirt—the proverbial brown nose. And she is a chewer. I made a nice little wooden stand so that she could lie down off the concrete pavement on the service patio. My intention was to round out the sharp corners, but in my eagerness to have her try out her platform bed, I allowed "Sam" to test the product. She quickly chewed the corners round. I couldn't have done it better with my electric saber saw. From the beginning, Samantha was to have been an outdoor dog, so I bought her a heavy-duty plastic doghouse for $75. She started doing some serious chewing on the corners of her doghouse. Will *jalapeño* pepper juice on the corners of her house be a deterrent?

Samantha is what's called a "mixed" breed. I've tried to figure out her lineage: she appears to have some black lab, her gray-booted legs indicate some spaniel heritage, and her Pointer ancestors come alive when she spots a bird and points at her prey with leg raised and bent. Trouble is, can't identify her oversized wagging tale. I thought I might be able to identify her basic lineage by running a test I discovered on the Internet. The site is www.emode.com. Check it out; it's a fun site. They have a series of psychological tests including: What is Your Emotional age? IQ Test; The Love Test; Are You High Maintenance? Are you Loony? Are You a Flirt? Celebrity Matchmaker. Is it Time to Break Up? Are You Sure Your Man's Straight? Are You a First Date Disaster? And many more. The one that caught my eye was: What Breed of Dog Are You? I thought maybe I could fill out Samantha's profile answering the multiple choice questions as if she were a person and thus be able to identify what breed of dog she is. I know this is goofy but not any goofier than "What Breed of Dog Are You." The test posed such questions as: At the dinner table (a) I use chopsticks; (b) I always use my best silver; (c) I always eat in front of the TV; (d) It's always meat and potatoes; (e) I pick at my food; (f) I lick my plate clean; (g) I tell lots of stories. This question was easy—Samantha licks her plate clean. In order to be fair to Samantha, I tested myself as well. I'm a Golden Retriever. Carol is an Irish Setter. Now admittedly there have been times when I wanted to return Samantha to Sandra with an explanation that it just isn't working out. I kept putting this off because every time I put Sam in the car headed for Sandra's house, Sam threw up. After determining that Samantha's profile classified her, too, as a Golden Retriever, I changed my mind. We Golden Retrievers have to stick together.

House Gets Painted

Our house isn't very old but it already has some stains on it and its cream color seems blah in comparison to other Guanajuato houses. Guanajuato houses are painted in blazing pinks, blues, purples, bright terracottas, and greens. We weren't ready for anything that dramatic, but we did want to add a little color to the place. I met a house painter that had just made a proposal to the building contractor who built and painted our home. The "signature" style of the painting crew who did our house seemed to more in the Jackson Pollock genre—paint drops on the floor. Although this new painter, Jésus, didn't get the bid for our neighbor's house, I learned that he had painted the Governor's mansion for the past three State governors, not a bad resume. His bid for me was 70 pesos per square meter, a little less than 70 cents per square foot, so I decided to hire him. He brought us a color chart of the hundreds of shades and tints offered by Comex, the Mexican paint company, and we ultimately chose B-08-5 for the exterior walls and H-06-6 for the trim. The trim "code" number was easy—dark blue to the green side. But describing the exterior wall code wasn't as easy. Jésus calls it salmon; looks pumpkin to me. The long and short of this Jésus story is that he and his crew did a fabulous job on our house, so good that I offered to recommend him to others. The rub came, however, that Jésus has no telephone, nor can he afford a truck. Business expansion here is difficult, if not impossible. A capitalized business loan carries a 40% interest charge by the bank.

Perhaps Jésus had all the business he could handle and all the employees he wanted, but it occurred to me that with very little capitalization he could expand his paint contractor's business. It seems a shame that Jésus and all the Jesúses in the developing nations are unable to realize their potential. World free trade and globalization would be far more beneficial if capital could somehow "trickle down" to these tiny businesses.

Millennium Arrives in Guanajuato

Beginning with Thanksgiving Day and culminating with New Year's Eve, the little group of Yankees, Canucks, and Brits that live here have delighted in a series of grand parties and feasts. Sure, some of us miss the snow, but there is something to be said for having cocktails served on the patio of Ron Mann and Sandra Ward's house prior to a sit-down Thanksgiving dinner. Or, the exquisite garden party at the *Casa de Espiritus Alegre* B&B that preceded Christmas, or an al fresco Christmas dinner for forty guests on the *terraza* at Montemayor's *Casa de Colibris*. Even the humming birds showed up for their Christmas Day feeding.

To celebrate the Millennium New Year's Eve, we were invited to the home of John and Mercedes Lichtwardt at *Colonia de Valenciana* that offers a panoramic of Guanajuato proper. We watched the annual New Year's celebrations on satellite TV, but as midnight approached we stepped outdoors to see the fireworks display from *Pipila* monument on the other side of town. We could see the lights of Silao, about 14 miles away, and Irapuato, about 27 miles. The bells of all of the churches rang out in unison to bring in the New Year and the New Millennium. It was a clear, star-filled night with the churches, aqueducts and other historic buildings of Guanajuato lit up below us. Albeit Guanajuato's fireworks display may not equal New York, London or Paris, we were proud of how beautiful our town looked.

In 1952, when I was the city planner in Green Bay, Wisconsin, I prepared a population forecast for the city. Thirty years was about as far as we usually would extrapolate population growth, and I remember chuckling over the idea of going out as far as the year 2000. How strange it sounded—Year 2000. I wondered if I would ever live long enough to see the next century and find out how our population projections had fared. How fortunate I am to have lived to celebrate this magical night, even if I haven't got the slightest recollection of what those population estimates were.

19

July 2000

Meeting with U.S. Consul

Members of the American community in Guanajuato met with American Consul Phil Maher at El Campo Viejo Restaurant on May 18, 2000. Charlie Montemayor arranged the luncheon meeting so that the consul could answer many of the questions we have concerning issues related to living in Mexico.

"The Colonel," as Consul Maher is known, has lived for thirty years in San Miguel, and has been America's consular agent for the last seventeen years. He was accompanied by his assistant, Paula Ramirez, who has worked for the consul for the last seven years, and who, according to the Colonel, "has answers for everything."

The session consisted mostly of questions from those in attendance and answers from the consul or his assistant, but, to begin, the Colonel briefly summarized what the American consul can and cannot do for Americans in Mexico.

What the Consul Can/Cannot Do:

(1) If you die in Mexico, the consul will inventory your property, will ship your body, and will do other tasks associated with clearing up your affairs.

(2) If you are a victim of a crime in Mexico, the consul can help you through the process of reporting the crime.

(3) If you are arrested in Mexico, the consul will visit you in jail, and will even bring you some of the necessities of life—towels, socks, soap, etc.

(4) The consul *cannot* represent you in a Mexican judicial proceeding, but he *can* help you pick a lawyer.

(5) The consul can arrange up to $200 for an emergency loan; and he can buy you a bus ticket to the border.

(6) If you're being abused by the Mexican legal system, the consul can make a complaint on your behalf through the American ambassador in Mexico City.

Absentee Voting:

Colonel Maher brought with him some "How To Vote" brochures and post-cards to request absentee ballots. Expatriates vote for President/Vice-President and U.S. senators and representatives in the state in which they last resided. State requirements vary for requesting a ballot, however, so the brochure is useful. You can get additional brochures and postcards from the consul's office in San Miguel.

Registration with the American Consul:

The consul also brought copies of a Registration Application, for those who are not already registered with his office. The form requires you to submit name and address information in Mexico, social security number(s), passport number(s), person(s) to contact in case of emergency, and other pertinent information. The consul advised that all American citizens, no matter how much time they spend in Mexico, should be registered with his office, but registration is strictly voluntary. If you haven't filled out this form, you are not registered, even if you've consulted the consul on other matters, such as FM3 renewals, etc.

Joan Romero, long time resident of Guanajuato who attended the meeting, also informed the group that residents of Guanajuato have also arranged for notification of next of kin in case of an accident or death. She has blank copies of the local form, should anyone be interested, which can be used as a backup to the consulate's form. The completed forms are sealed for privacy, and Joan keeps them at her home. They are only opened in case of emergency.

Questions and Answers

LABOR LAW, DOMESTIC HELP CONTRACTS

If you employ household help, it is advisable to have a formal contract for the work performed. The consul brought a sample contract, which was drawn up by a Guanajuato attorney.

Who Is Covered?

If your employee works more than 4 hours per day *and* more than 20 hours per week, s/he is covered by Mexico's labor law. Otherwise, s/he is not. Employees doing a time-limited project are not covered under the labor law. Paula suggested that it is a good idea to get a copy of the law, known as the *Ley de Trabajo,* (Labor Law).

Christmas Bonus (The *aguinaldo.*)

The *aguinaldo* is the equivalent of 2 weeks' wages, and it applies to everyone, whether they are covered under the Labor Law or not. There are no exceptions. It must be paid on or before December 20 in any year.

Vacation and Vacation Bonus. Employees are entitled to receive from 3 to 16 days of vacation per year (or a pro-rated number of vacation days, if the employee does not work full-time).

NO. OF VACATION DAYS

Year 1	3 days
Year 2	6 days
Year 3	8 days
Year 4	8 days
Year 5	8 days
Year 6	10 days
Year 7	10 days
Year 8	12 days
Year 9	12 days
Year 10	14 days
Year 11	14 days
Year 12	16 days

In other words, after the fourth year of employment, an additional 2 days of vacation are earned every second year, up to a total of 16 days, beginning in year 12. You are also required to pay a *vacation bonus*, which is 25 percent over and above the employee's regular salary.

Social Security.

You are obligated to put your employee on Social Security if their employment is covered under the Ley de Trabajo. For domestics who work in your home, the only social security benefits they will receive will be medical insurance for themselves and for their children.

If you are constructing a house, or doing major remodeling, make sure you have a written contract with your contractor/builder that states that s/he will make social security payments for the laborers on the project.

Obligations to a Long-Term Employee.

What are your obligations if your employee can't work for medical reasons? That depends on whether the illness is job-related or not job-related. The two scenarios present very different circumstances. If the injury is job-related and if the employee is on Social Security, then their medical costs are already covered (see above). If the injury is job-related and they're not on Social Security, then you are responsible for all medical expenses.

Firing an Employee.

If you lay someone off for cause, you'd better be able to prove the cause. For example, if an employee is caught stealing, you should go to the office of the *Procruraría General* (attorney general) to make a formal complaint. If, on the other hand, you want to fire someone for laziness, then you should write a letter to the employee and send a copy of the letter to the Labor Court. The letter should give the employee, say, 30 days to straighten up. If after 30 days, the employee still has not improved, write another letter and send another copy to the Court. Finally, after the second 30-day period, let the Labor Court take care of it. In other words, build a paper trail.

WILLS

Should I Have a U.S. or a Mexican Will?

The consul advises that you have one or the other, but not both. The standard Mexican will includes a clause that states that all previous wills are null and void. If you engage a Mexican attorney, make sure he is aware of this, especially if you also have a U.S. will. Maher advises: If most of your assets are in the U.S., have a U.S. will. If most of your assets are in Mexico, have a Mexican will. There exists an international treaty that allows Mexico to follow the wishes of your U.S. will, and vice-versa.

Beyond the issue of whether to have a U.S. or a Mexican will, for some things you should also make use of a letter of instruction to your executor, rather than leaving these details in your will. For example, if you want to be cremated, put that information in a letter of instruction. Another example might be if you want to leave a CD to a servant. Putting that information in a letter of instruction would speed up the process of getting that money more rapidly into the hands of the individual.

The consul also noted that he has seen tragic consequences for "significant others," in the event of death. They have no legal status, so he advises that if you have a significant other, "do something to legalize your situation."

Death

First of all, many of us have heard the story that, in the event of death, in Mexico you *must* be buried within 24 hours. The fact is that in Mexico you *can't* be buried within 24 hours of death without a special certificate. The 24-hour burial story is a myth.

In the event of death, the consul needs: (1) the deceased's passport, (2) the deceased's social security number, and (3) a Mexican death certificate (which can be obtained from the *Registro Civil*). If you use an undertaker, part of his job will be to obtain the death certificate, signed by the attending physician. Many Americans who die in Mexico wish to be cremated. There is no crematorium in Guanajuato, but there are crematoriums in León, Irapuato, and San Miguel. If arrangements are made with them, they'll pick up the body and take care of the death certificate. Concerning the death certificate, we are advised to ask for lots of copies—perhaps twice as many as what we think we'll need. The deceased ashes should be brought to the consulate, where they will be sealed, and he will prepare a Mortuary Certificate, which gives permission to take the sealed box out of country. The consul advises that ashes have also been mailed and that the charge is nominal (about US $17-$18). The consul will also notify the Social Security Administration, the Veteran's Administration, and other pertinent government agencies, via a U.S. government official form, "Report of Death for American Citizen Abroad." This is because, in most U.S. jurisdictions, a Mexican death certificate will not be acceptable.

After death, household goods can be sold, given away, or sent back to U.S. To return household goods to the U.S. after death, or even if you're still living, you need: (1) an FM3, (2) a U.S. passport, and (3) an inventory of possessions. The cost for the paperwork is US $55.00, paid to the consul.

MEXICAN HEALTH INSURANCE

U.S. citizens are eligible for Mexican health insurance. Any resident of Mexico, whether a Mexican citizen or a foreign national, is eligible. You simply pay an annual fee. Sometimes they might ask for a medical report.

If you're trying to get insurance for a married couple, you need to show a marriage certificate. As for many legal documents, these are only accepted as valid in Mexico if they are accompanied by an *apostille*, as well as an official translation. An *apostille*, essentially, is a document that verifies the legality of the signatures on your original document. For example, if you have a job teaching English in Mexico, you must present a notarized copy of your Bachelor's degree. The *apostille*, obtained from the office of the secretary of state in the state in which you obtained your degree and/or in which it was notarized, simply attests that the notary is officially registered in that state and that his/her signature, attesting to the validity of the original document, is also valid. In the case of a marriage certificate, the same process would apply. The secretary of state in the state in which you were married would attest, via the *apostille*, to the validity of the signatories to the marriage certificate.

IMMIGRATION ISSUES

FM3 Renewals.

You can begin the renewal process up to 30 days before the expiration date on your FM3. It is possible to renew for someone else, under emergency circumstances; the final decision about whether to allow renewal *in absencia* rests with immigration officials.

Advantages and Disadvantages of FM2.

If you are at least 55 years of age and have held an FM3 continuously for five years, you are eligible for an FM2. Income requirements are a bit higher than for the FM3, and the biggest drawback is that you can't be out of the country for more than 90 days total for each year of the first 3 years of the FM2. After 5 years, however, you don't have to renew an FM2 anymore. You can also own an American car only for the first 5 years of your FM2.

Can You Take an Employee (Domestic Help) to the States?

Yes, but you must take full responsibility for the employee while s/he is in U.S. Mexican immigration grants the travel visa for the employee, which is usually good for 3 months. Whether the visa will be approved is a matter of judgment; in most cases, Immigration will approve it.

How Do I Start a Business in Mexico?

That answer is complicated and depends upon many factors. If you want to start a business, it's best to consult with the consul in person.

Can I Ply a Trade or Profession for Money?

The short answer is "yes." Once again, consult the consul. The Colonel also suggests that you disclose all the volunteer work or creative work that you do in Mexico, so it can be listed on your FM3.

CARS

When Do I Renew My Car's Sticker?

You do not have to renew your car's sticker every year. As long as your FM3 is in order, you can continue to drive on the car's original sticker. Problems on this issue have been created because of an intra-agency fight between *Hacienda,* (Treasury) and *Aduana,* (Customs). The issue has since been resolved in favor of not renewing your sticker.

Who Can Drive My Car?

There is also disagreement among agencies on this issue and cars have been confiscated, although, to date, all have eventually been returned. It is best, however, if only the FM3 holder, their spouse, and their children drive the vehicle. Both spouses must be on the title for the car.

What Should I Do if I Have an Accident?

You should (1) have proof of insurance; (2) only carry *copies* of documents in your car, not originals; (3) call the traffic police for the jurisdiction you're in (i.e., city, state, or federal, depending on who maintains the road where the accident occurred); and (4) always settle on the spot, even in the presence of the police, if you can.

MEXICAN DIVORCE

A Mexican divorce usually takes 30 days if both parties are able to reach an economic agreement. Otherwise, it can go on for years. Mexican courts tend not to favor the woman in divorce proceedings.

Author's Note: The information contained in this Newsletter is based on information given in 2000. Rules and regulations change over time. It is provided to the reader as a guideline only. It is always advisable to confirm any action you may take with the American Consular Agency in San Miguel de Allende.

Epilogue
Lessons Learned

A few years ago, I read an article in *The New York Times* about a survey conducted by the B'Nai Brith in which Americans were asked which races and nationalities they held in the highest esteem. I think the English came out at the very top; Jews, who had been down some in earlier polls, were now ranked somewhere around seventh. But what struck me rather hurtfully, because I am an American of Mexican decent, is that Mexicans were next to the bottom. I don't have any quarrel with the accuracy of the survey. When you're next to the bottom there is no point in quibbling about any statistical sampling errors. Nevertheless, what I saw in this survey didn't jibe with my own personal experience.

I was born and grew up in Janesville, Wisconsin, a town about forty miles southeast of Madison and one hundred miles northwest of Chicago. Both of my parents were born in the State of Coahuila, which is in the north of Mexico. My Mother (Elvira Villarreal), a young schoolteacher, married my Father, who had been educated in Mexico by private tutors and later attended business schools in the United States. Each of their parents were respected, well-off by Mexico standards at the time, but not rich. They left Mexico because they found conditions during the 1910 Mexican revolution intolerable. First the revolutionaries would raid them, and then the government forces would raid them. This happened over and over again with each side requisitioning horses, cattle, crops and money; and it was not without some danger to their lives. The two warring factions took what they wanted in exchange for worthless chits. I don't think my Mother or my Father were particularly political but they wanted out.

My Father was invited to come to Janesville by George S. Parker, a Janesville telegraph operator who invented the fountain pen and went on to found the Parker Pen Company. Parker was a visionary businessman who as early as the 1920's was a strong advocate of foreign export. He built an export department with native-speaking business people who were able to correspond in the language of the country Parker Pen was doing business. My Dad handled Mexico and Central America. The company's export strategy and an excellent product resulted in great success for Parker Pen. My Father remained employed throughout the depression when businesses of all kinds were laying people off or closing down.

I was the youngest of four boys and two girls in our family. I think we were the only Mexican family in Janesville at the time, and my memories are that my family was welcomed by all of Janesville. The Parkers, in particular, took an interest in our family inviting us to their home to swim in their pool or to listen to classical music in the music room and just visit. My older brothers and sisters were all high achievers—in dance, acting, music, art, writing, oratory, and above all academic achievement. These attributes didn't always include me, but some of my siblings' luster may have rubbed off—along with some high expectations, often difficult to reach. The Janesville parents wanted their children to play with the Montemayor kids perhaps with the notion that their children would benefit by the association, but who knows, maybe we were all contaminated in the process. I can remember hearing about mothers who wanted their daughters to go out with my older brother although this didn't happen in my case. A few years ago I met the now-grown daughter of a well-known University of Wisconsin Philosophy Professor who said as a child some fifty-five years ago she yearned to be exactly like my two sisters because of their dancing and artistic abilities. My sisters both married professors of philosophy at the university.

It's this background that makes it hard for me to understand the apparent low esteem that Americans have for Mexicans. It didn't seem to be the case with my family although I do recall on occasion feeling that we weren't real Americans; somehow, we were different. Porfirio Diaz, long time president/dictator of Mexico, once said of the Mexican-Americans: "Ah, the poor Mexican-Americans—in Mexico, they are not Mexicans and alas, in America, they are not Americans." My brother Gus, was killed in World War II. That may have been the defining moment when I decided we were just as much American as our blond, blue-eyed neighbors with their German and Norwegian names. The price was too high, however, just to convince myself of what should have been obvious all along.

Here in Guanajuato, the Americans, Canadians and English that we know admire the Mexicans: "What marvelous people," is often heard. I've heard this same view held in other parts of Mexico where English-speaking people live—almost the exact opposite of what the B'Nai Brith survey revealed. One would think that the qualities of the Mexican people, as we who live here have come to know, would have a special appeal to Americans: hard working, close families, polite, cheerful, helpful, personally immaculately clean and unbelievably generous. Is it the movies that give us the unfavorable image—dirty, poor, lazy, backward, cruel, and dishonest, or is it ignorance? Perhaps some of both, but I think ignorance takes top honors here: the same unthinking blindness that fuels prejudice toward any nationality or race that is different from one's own.

So why and how did Carole and I decide to move to Mexico? Some people have asked if I was trying to find my "roots." I don't think so. My roots are my family. Going back ten or fifteen generations to chase down a forbear can be fun and interesting and I'm all for it but I don't think it says a lot about who I am. After all, I don't believe that my family tree is a single incestuous vertical line; there are a lot of different contributions that went in to making me who I am.

Of one thing I am absolutely certain: my positive childhood memories and the experiences of living in Mexico for seven years have proved the fallacies an prejudice about the Mexican people are just that—fallacies and prejudice. One has only to experience this marvelous country and her people to quickly know that here is a unique civilization, a nation whose history is rich, whose national pride is unquestioned, whose people have contributed much to the beauty and culture of the entire world.

We continue to live and enjoy our retirement in Mexico. My email address is: charlymont@int.com.mx and our website is: http://clik.to/charlymont.

0-595-29281-X